An EXTREME GOD *for An* EXTREME LIFE

APRIL CHAPMAN

Unless otherwise indicated, all Scripture references are taken from the Holy Bible, New Living Translation, copyright © 1996, 2004, 2015 by Tyndale House Foundation. Used by permission of Tyndale House Publishers, Inc., Carol Stream, Illinois 60188. All rights reserved.

Scripture references marked MSG are taken from The Message. Copyright © 1993, 1994, 1995, 1996, 2000, 2001, 2002. Used by permission of NavPress Publishing Group.

Scripture references marked NIV are taken from THE HOLY BIBLE, NEW INTERNATIONAL VERSION®, NIV® Copyright © 1973, 1978, 1984, 2011 by Biblica, Inc.® Used by permission. All rights reserved worldwide.

Scripture references marked NKJV are taken from the New King James Version®. Copyright © 1982 by Thomas Nelson. Used by permission. All rights reserved.

Scripture references marked KJV are taken from the King James Version®.

Scripture references marked GWT are taken from GOD'S WORD®, © 1995 God's Word to the Nations. Used by permission of Baker Publishing Group.

Italics in Scripture quotations have been added by the author for emphasis.

Library of Congress Control Number 2018910811

Cover Picture by Voula Vatsinea

ISBN: 978-1-7327854-0-3
ISBN eBook: 978-1-7327854-1-0
Published by Abundant Joy Publishing

Dedication

This book is dedicated to my daughters, Jerilyn, Ainsley and Daisy, who make every battle worth fighting.

Contents

For everything there is a season,

   a time for every activity under heaven.
A time to be born and a time to die.

   A time to plant and a time to harvest.
A time to kill and a time to heal.

   A time to break down and a time to build.
A time to cry and a time to laugh.

   A time to grieve and a time to dance.
A time to scatter stones and a time to gather stones.

   A time to embrace and a time to turn away.
A time to search and a time to quit searching.

   A time to keep and a time to throw away.
A time to tear and a time to mend.

   A time to be quiet and a time to speak.
A time to love and a time to hate.

   A time for war and a time for peace.

~ Ecclesiastes 3: 1-8

Introduction

Oh, how I would have loved to write a book about the life I dreamed about as a little girl. Instead, you hold the book about the life I never wanted, never planned, and certainly never expected—the life which included a naïve, young Christian girl marrying a psychopath, adopting a special needs child, fighting the legal system for a decade, and somehow figuring out that those storms taught me more about God's love than my dream life ever would have.

God first planted the idea of writing a book in my heart many years ago, although at the time I had no idea what I would be writing about. Then I had to go live the life God would use to grow my faith. When He finally said it was time to start writing, I conveniently reminded Him that I had no idea how to structure the book, because in my entire life no one has *ever* described me as organized. I prayed about it and expected an answer in a few months because I was in no rush to start. Three days later, I read the following passage from Ecclesiastes 3: 1-8.

> *For everything there is a season,*
> > *a time for every activity under heaven.*
> *A time to be born and a time to die.*
> > *A time to plant and a time to harvest.*
> *A time to kill and a time to heal.*
> > *A time to break down and a time to build.*
> *A time to cry and a time to laugh.*
> > *A time to grieve and a time to dance.*

A time to scatter stones and a time to gather stones.

A time to embrace and a time to turn away.

A time to search and a time to quit searching.

A time to keep and a time to throw away.

A time to tear and a time to mend.

A time to be quiet and a time to speak.

A time to love and a time to hate.

A time for war and a time for peace.

When I finished reading it, I felt the Holy Spirit say, *Read it again.* So, I read it again. Nothing. When I finished it the second time, I felt that still small voice say to my spirit...*Read. It. Again.* I read it slowly the third time and related ideas started popping into my head with each phrase. As I read "a time to be born," the idea of physical birth, spiritual birth, and the birth of a dream came to mind. This elaboration continued throughout the entire passage. At the end, I realized God had just given me the structure for my book! This is why each chapter is titled with a phrase from this passage. The chapters are placed in alphabetical order, because that's how the story needed to be told.

Each chapter includes personal stories, biblical truths and questions to help apply those truths to your own life. My prayer for you is that your heart will be encouraged to trust God through whatever challenges you face. Your struggles may be different than mine, but we all know what it feels like to be overwhelmed and desperate for God to rescue us from our circumstances, our enemies or even ourselves.

When you finish each chapter, I hope you feel as if we are becoming better and better friends. We may have yet to meet, but I hope to one day, if not here, then in heaven. For now, these pages will have to do.

1

A Time to Be Born

I was nine months pregnant when Hurricane Frances swept across the state of Florida on September 5, 2004, heading straight toward Tampa and my family. As luck would have it, the barometric pressure dropped enough to put my overdue body into labor. My husband and I got in the car and headed to the hospital. Oh, wait. We weren't going to a hospital; we were going to a birth center, which had sounded like a great plan when envisioning a perfect birth. However, when facing a hurricane with 145 mph winds, my birth center looked like a tiny house surrounded by a few too many giant trees.

We drove through the wind and rain, carefully navigating the already fallen trees. When we arrived, I was in full-blown labor, and we had no other option but to just push through. *(Pun intended, of course.)* I'd chosen a natural birth with my first daughter and assumed this second birth would be just as wonderful. Never. Assume. Anything. First off, this time it hurt...*worse*. All I kept thinking was *Get me that epidural,* only I didn't have access to an epidural at a birth center with a midwife.

No water. No electricity. Definitely no epidural. And finally, no hospital since roads were blocked and I'm pretty sure the ambulances were otherwise engaged. As the eye of the hurricane passed over us and the distinct stillness of the winds saturated our senses, Daisy Marie entered our world. The traumatic experience wasn't over yet, though, because she was blue and not breathing. The earth stopped spinning while we waited for her first breath. Finally, her beautiful cry erupted. Daisy was here, all 9.1 pounds of her. Yes...ouch.

We all enter this world after hanging out in a womb until it is our *time to be born*. For some, like Daisy, the birth is filled with drama. For others, like my best friend Misty, it means a baby arriving early as a tiny four-pounder resembling a drowned rat. Her words, not mine. Every birth experience is unique and life-changing.

We don't choose how or when we come into this world, but there is no question that we were *chosen* to come. God chose each of us specifically. It is a relief to know none of us is an accident, at least not in God's eyes, even if our parents jokingly call us one!

SPIRITUAL BIRTH DAY

Although we have no say in how and when we are physically born, we do get to determine if we are reborn.

> *Jesus replied, "I tell you the truth, unless you are born again, you cannot see the Kingdom of God."*
>
> *"What do you mean?" exclaimed Nicodemus. "How can an old man go back into his mother's womb and be born again?"*
>
> *Jesus replied, "I assure you, no one can enter the Kingdom of God without being born of water and the Spirit. Humans can reproduce only human life, but the Holy Spirit gives birth to spiritual life. So don't be surprised when I say, 'You must be born again' (John 3: 3-7, NLT).*

We experience the joy and privilege of being born again once we choose to start our life with our awesome heavenly Father. Interestingly, as men and women pursue each other, which can result in physical birth, our heavenly Father pursues us, which leads to our spiritual birth.

We can't remember our physical birth, but we don't forget our spiritual birthday. I was a little lady of six. I remember telling my parents I was ready to ask Jesus into my heart and wanted to walk down the aisle in church on Sunday. When Sunday came around, I could hardly wait until the end of the sermon and, as soon as they started the weekly invitation hymn, I popped out of the pew and headed to the front. My pastor prayed with me, and I immediately felt a huge weight being lifted off my shoulders, leaving me feeling light and free. Even at six, I was amazed because I couldn't remember ever feeling a weight until it was suddenly gone.

God uses us, persistent sinners saved by grace, to reach out to a hurting world.

I will never forget that moment, but do you know what I love most about it? It is the fact that I never doubt or question whether I was saved. It's as clear to me as the fact that the sun will rise tomorrow. God our Father wants us to be confident of our salvation. If you aren't confident, seek Him and lay down those fears once and for all.

BIRTH OF A DREAM

Once our foundation with God is secure, we find He places new dreams in our hearts. When a dream is born, it begins with intense excitement and passion. It may feel lofty or even slightly impossible, if there is such a thing as "slightly" impossible. You may want to tell everyone you know about it, or you may want to treasure and ponder it in your heart.

However, I believe God plants a dream when our hearts beat in unison with His. God uses us, persistent sinners saved by grace, to reach out to a hurting world. The dream God gave me was to write and speak, encouraging women to trust God enough to experience hope in this often tumultuous life.

Your dream may be to...

Become a nurse,

Home-school your children,

Complete your college education,

Be in full-time ministry, or

Start a business.

Whatever dream God plants, we are guaranteed He will be faithful to complete it in us. Sometimes the biggest obstacle to our dream is *us*. We are so limited in our thinking that we cannot think big enough for what God wants for us. But we can ask God to remove the limitations and give us a full view of His vision.

The birth of dreams is only the beginning of the good things God has planned. Hang on to the excitement a new birth brings. Ride it out through the gestation until we see it come to fruition. Oh, how exciting life is for those who live out the dreams God has for them!

Oh, how exciting life is for those who live out the dreams God has for them!

When I was young, my dreams consisted of finishing college, getting married and having a baby. For years, those were my only dreams in life. I figured once those were accomplished, Jesus could come back...but I thought if He could wait until then, it would be awesome. You may have some future plans that make you hope Jesus waits a little longer to return as well.

A glorious truth about God is that, once a dream has come to fruition, we are soon filled with the exciting birth of another dream. After having my family, God birthed in me a new desire to serve Him in women's ministry. God confirmed His plan for me when I met Maureen, my new neighbor, who would become one of my best friends. Within a few days of meeting Maureen, God prompted me to share my dreams with her. She encouraged me and shared the heart she and her husband had to someday minister to young families. Needless to say, we immediately connected and I knew God not only put us together, but also confirmed my new path.

Some of us are blessed with good friends who encourage our dreams, but we also have an enemy who doesn't want to see our dreams come true and will try to place barriers along the way. Don't let those deter you. The harder Satan fights, the more glory God receives when the battle is won.

My dream of ministering to women through writing and speaking began at the Birth of a Dream stage, and now it has come to fruition. There is no reason why you can't see a dream through to completion as well. Dream big and watch God move on your behalf!

Make It Personal

1. What are the dreams God has placed in your heart? If none come to mind, pray and challenge yourself to be open to whatever dream God plants.

2. How can you move closer to accomplishing your dream right now?

3. Have you had a spiritual birthday? What do you remember most about it?

2

A Time to Break Down

One of my family's favorite television shows was *ABC's Extreme Home Makeover*, which chose a deserving family and built a new house for them in seven days. These houses were amazing with all of the newest gadgets and conveniences. However, before a new home could be built, the current home with all of its failures had to be torn down. It always seemed like the crew enjoyed demolition day, maybe because the destruction was clearing the way for a blessing.

At times, I feel the need for a demolition day to tear down things I've constructed in my life which offer no value or no longer serve the purpose for which they were originally intended. Pride would definitely be a big one for me. Pride is the root of almost all sin, and it continues to find new ways to infiltrate my life. As soon as I humble myself in one area, my pride starts popping up in another, reminding me of the Whac-A-Mole game found in those annoying kid arcades. Pride rears its ugly head, and I feel a *"whack"*…followed by the humbling of my spirit and circumstances.

Pride in my marriage…whack…divorce.

Pride in my financial status….whack…poverty.

Pride in my independence…whack…cry for help.

Pride in my parenting…whack…prodigal child.

I've also had to demolish discipline techniques that no longer work with my kids, or more accurately, probably never worked. For instance, before my daughter Jerilyn was diagnosed with autism, I thought spanking was a good consequence for her misbehavior since it had worked as a deterrent for me when I was growing up. However, I quickly discovered spanking wasn't achieving the desired results with Jerilyn, because she was continuing in the same behaviors without connecting the cause and effect.

I felt the Holy Spirit tell me to broaden my discipline techniques and avoid spanking as an option for a few months. I needed to break down my methods of approaching behavior problems. This led me to research and find many great books, including *Creative Correction* by Lisa Welchel which is still one of my favorites.

I incorporated more creative techniques like telling relatable stories to teach a lesson, or as she got older, having her write out verses or sentences addressing the behavior. A drop of hot sauce on a lying tongue worked because she didn't like it, which is a good thing when you are looking for consequences. Sometimes, we have to think outside of the box or re-evaluate what we learned from our family of origin in order to demolish ineffective approaches and find the right solution.

WHY, OH WHY, DO WE DO THE THINGS WE DO?

A daughter once asked her mother why she cut off the ends of the ham before she cooked it, and her mother admitted that she didn't know the reason, she just knew that was how her mother had always done it. So, the mother went to her mother (the grandmother) and asked why she cut off the ends of the ham. Her mother said she didn't know the reason, but *her* mom had always done it. So, they asked her mom (the great-grandmother) why she always cut off the ends of the ham before she cooked it. She replied, "I don't know why *you* do it, but I did it because otherwise the ham wouldn't fit into my pan."

All of these women were continuing a behavior from generation to generation without having any understanding as to why they did it.

I often find myself hanging on to my way of doing something or even my way of thinking about something for way too long, a lot of times without even knowing why. I'm not a super analytical person, but there are times when I force myself to sit down and analyze why I do certain things and whether my reasons are valid.

While married to an emotionally abusive man, I walked around on eggshells, scared to bring up certain topics, even practicing how to say something a hundred times in my head before actually speaking. Eventually, I stopped sharing my thoughts and dreams because I couldn't trust them in his hands.

I started building up walls around my heart to protect it and learned to close off my emotions. My friends nicknamed me "the robot," because of this ability—or disability, depending on how you look at it—to shut down my feelings. I've since discovered that this response has a name...*dissociation*.

Cynthia Henrie, MFT, describes dissociation as "a defense mechanism that everyone uses every day. In its most common form, mild dissociation includes daydreaming, 'zoning out,' or doing things on 'autopilot.'...Trauma and abuse survivors often rely too heavily on dissociation as a defense mechanism...If you are able to function without fully experiencing the emotional impact of an event, you can accomplish tasks until it is safer to deal with your emotions." For me, dissociation shows up in the ability to turn off my emotions.

Ironically, if you read books about how to survive in an unhealthy relationship, they will actually teach you to try to disconnect emotionally. Basically, the recommendation is that you not take everything to heart as a way of coping.

However, what had been a coping mechanism for me became a problem once the desire to be in another relationship arose. I couldn't turn it off and force myself to feel connected emotionally again. I eventually realized breaking down these walls was necessary if I hoped to ever give and receive love freely.

Once the problem was identified, I tried to figure out the best way to solve it. Telling myself to connect to my feelings didn't work. Talking it out with my girlfriends didn't work, although not for lack of trying. Thank God I have such patient girlfriends! A traditional Christian counselor didn't work either, but it did lead me down the right path.

My Christian counselor identified PTSD, Post Traumatic Stress Disorder, which can happen to anyone who experiences a traumatic event or a persistent stress. The counselor suggested EMDR therapy. She explained EMDR, Eye-Movement Desensitization and Reprocessing, as a therapy using bilateral stimulation. This is accomplished by forcing a person to engage both sides of the brain consistently, which causes the brain to rewire itself instead of closing down the emotional side.

Admittedly, when she mentioned this, my response was, "Sure, I'll look into it," the same way I tell my kids "I'll think about it" after they ask me to do something we all know I'm probably never going to let them do. It actually took a few more months before I was willing to start exploring EMDR. Lo and behold, research had proven it successful, and I felt a little spark of hope that I might be fixable...at least in this area.

I was able to look forward to the future, whatever it held, and let go of the past that had been holding me hostage.

After finding an EMDR therapist, I started weekly sessions. She gave me headphones to wear and sensors to hold in my hands. The headphones would alternately beep from right to left, and the sensors would send alternating pulses as well. Then she told me to allow my mind to go wherever it wanted to go as she asked me open-ended questions. Can I just say...scary? After a few minutes, she would ask me if I wanted to share anything. *Wanted* might be pushing it; *reluctant but willing* was more accurate.

One of the most telling questions my therapist asked me was what mental picture appeared when she said the word "marriage." The image that came to my mind instantly was crystal clear...a jail cell. After that session, I took a poll among my married friends, asking what picture came to their minds. Their answers were things like "a heart with a lock to which my husband holds the key," or "a vision of my husband and me walking hand in hand down a path into our future." *No one* said "jail cell."

Apparently, I had veered just a bit off the path of "healthy" and needed to tear down that image. The therapist asked me to consider what God says marriage should be, and whether my previous experience was really a marriage based on what God intended.

Of course, the technical answer is yes, I had been legally married. However, I started to think about what God says about marriage.

> *A cord of three strands is not easily broken (Ecclesiastes 4:12).*
>
> *Thou shalt not commit adultery (Exodus 20:14).*
>
> *A man should treasure the wife of his youth (Proverbs 5:18).*
>
> *Love is kind. It does not envy. It does not boast. It is not self-seeking (1 Corinthians 13:4).*
>
> *A husband needs to love his wife like Christ loved the church and gave himself up for it (Ephesians 5:25).*

Needless to say, these verses had not been my experience of marriage.

It is amazing that such simple communication tools started to connect my thoughts and feelings to each other again. EMDR therapy helped me not just know in my head, but also feel in my heart that a marriage with a godly man could be a totally different experience. It wouldn't be perfect, because no marriage is, but it could be something that brought joy to my life. Once I broke down the jail cell image in my mind, I was able to look forward to the future, whatever it held, and let go of the past that had been holding me hostage.

Christ came so that we may be free, and free indeed. Being real with our feelings and with our selves brings freedom. It means we experience the highs and lows, but there is a joy in embracing both honestly, the way we were designed to before trauma distorted everything.

What is holding you back from experiencing the full measure of joy in your life? It may be you need to tear down a barrier. If you are like me, you may have attempted the demolition on your own without much success. Ask God to come in and do the demo work. Depending on what it is, He may actually call in a whole crew to come in and help. That's okay, the important thing is acknowledging *A Time to Break Down* so you can move on to the next step, *A Time to Build Up.*

> *Some of you will rebuild the deserted ruins of your cities. Then you will be known as a rebuilder of walls and a restorer of homes (Isaiah 58:12).*

Make It Personal

1. If your heart had a demolition day, what would you break down?

2. What are some coping mechanisms you've used to help you deal with difficult times or traumatic experiences in your life?

3. What is holding you back from experiencing the full measure of joy in your life?

3

A Time to Build Up

As women, we are held to near impossible standards of perfection. Every time we see a magazine cover with a model wearing a size zero or turn on the television to watch the wonder woman who appears to manage work, family and beauty perfectly, we die a little inside. Okay, maybe we don't die, but our self-esteem takes a big hit.

The truth is often buried under lies. The model who is already eating-disorder-skinny is airbrushed to be even thinner, and the television star has a whole crew of make-up artists, personal trainers and scriptwriters working to make her look perfect. Goodness, if I could write scripts my children had to follow, my day would look "perfect" too! I can imagine it now…

> *"Good morning, sweet daughter."*
>
> *"Good morning, Mother, I woke up this morning thinking about how lucky I am to have you. I was wondering if there is anything I could do today that would make your life a little easier?"*

Yes, I would make a wonderful TV mom. Unfortunately, my real life is the version where I wake up grumpy children, make sure they eat healthy meals, play constant chauffeur and break up fights before they escalate to wars. When I'm not doing those things, I am purposefully building up my daughters' self-esteem by reminding them they are beautiful, smart and funny in a culture that is intent upon making them feel the opposite. I find it easy to speak those truths over my children, but there are days when I struggle to believe them about myself. As women, we walk into the battlefield of self-perception every day.

I often feel weighed down accomplishing the endless daily tasks and easily lose focus of the dreams God has planted in my heart. Feeling depleted of all energy, time and resources brings me to a place of desperately needing God to build me up. At times, I need Him to do this so I can make it through the day. At other times, it's so I can truly believe in my ability to accomplish my dreams. I forget God is my Abba Father, or Daddy, and He desires to build me up.

> *And now I entrust you to God and the message of his grace that is able to build you up and give you an inheritance with all those he has set apart for himself (Acts 20:32).*

We often forget we are the daughters of a King. Let's remind ourselves what God thinks about us…

> *He knit us together in the womb (Psalm 139:13).*
>
> *Our name is written on the palm of His hand (Isaiah 49:16).*
>
> *He desires to give good gifts to His children (Matthew 7:11).*
>
> *We can do ALL things through Christ, who gives us strength (Philippians 4:13).*
>
> *He wants to give us the desires of our heart (Psalm 37:4).*
>
> *God makes ALL things possible (Matthew 19:26).*

In light of these truths, it's impossible for me to say I can't do something if God has called me to it. Following my divorce, I was anxious about reentering the work force after being at home with my children for the previous six years. During the times when I doubted my abilities, God used His Word and godly women in my life to build me up. I was hired by a company, where I gained the technical knowledge and developed the connections I needed to take the next step towards my dream of becoming a professional speaker.

Another year down the road, God opened the door for me to create my own company, speaking at conferences and offering consulting to local businesses. This was a bigger leap of faith and required me to build up a steady stream of business. Ten years earlier, I would never have imagined myself as an entrepreneur. God has an amazing way of expanding our imaginations.

BUILD UP YOUR GIRLFRIENDS

I am blessed to have wonderfully encouraging friends and pray I am the same kind of friend to them. God has given us the command to "encourage one another" (Hebrews 10:25). We all desire encouragement from our friends, whether it's about our newest weight loss idea, our latest parenting approach, or getting involved in a ministry to which we feel God is calling us.

I met one of my closest friends, Julie, through our involvement in starting a ministry together. While we were still acquaintances, she mentioned she felt the Lord was leading her to start a ladies' Bible study. She told me the biggest hurdle for her was going to be teaching. She could see herself administrating the study, but couldn't envision actually teaching it. My excitement was immediate, and I said I could see myself teaching, but I surely couldn't see myself administrating a study. Our YMCA Women's Bible Study was born. I could write a whole book about our Bible study group, but I will simply share

We often forget we are daughters of a King.

the ironic fact that, with a little encouragement, Julie ended up teaching as well, since God grew the group so quickly. She proved to be an excellent teacher destined for women's ministry.

Needing encouragement is universal. Sometimes, the need is critical. The more women I know, the more I understand everyone experiences hardships and needs encouragement to help make it through. I experienced some days, especially as a single parent, where I had to "phone a friend" from my closet where I was hiding from the chaos. I was desperate with a single plea…"Talk me down, or these children are going to take me down!"

Encouragement can come in the form of…

…a thoughtful gift

…a phone call

…an email

…a lunch date

…a prayer.

My friend Francine is one of my best encouragers. I can call her when I'm at my lowest and know that within a few minutes she will lift me up. She speaks God's Word over my life, the fruit of the lifetime she has spent seeking the Lord's presence. She is grounded in her faith and in God's faithfulness. Francine understands life is not always "good," but God is. We all need a "Francine" in our lives. Be the encourager for someone in your life.

BUILD UP OTHERS

> *Do not let any unwholesome talk come out of your mouths, but only what is helpful for building others up according to their needs, that it may benefit those who listen (Ephesians 4:29, NIV).*

As Christians we are commanded to encourage and build up others according to their needs…not ours. Think of all the people with whom we interact on a regular basis: parents, spouses, children, co-workers, neighbors, church members, friends and strangers. Who in our lives needs us to come alongside them and build them up?

A friend called me after a big fight with her husband. As we discussed it together, one thing became clear: her husband felt she was overly critical and didn't respect him. I've been on both ends of that experience…as the one being overly critical and as the one on the receiving end of a critical spirit. I find, fairly consistently, that criticism does the opposite of what was intended. It pushes people away and rarely brings anything beneficial to a relationship.

Criticism makes us part of the problem instead of the solution.

I'm not implying we shouldn't address difficulties in a relationship, but rather, we should approach them with wisdom. The old saying, "You can catch more flies with honey than with vinegar" is often true in communication. I believe this is why God gives us this warning:

> *Better to live in a desert than with a quarreling and angry woman (Proverbs 21:19, GW).*

The good news is that we can choose *not* to be that woman, even when we see an area in another's life where change is needed. While criticism can be an easy go-to response when we see sin in someone's life, our criticism makes us part of the problem instead of the solution. When my daughters are facing a difficult person or situation, I often tell them, "Don't let *their* sin become *your* sin." Basically, don't let someone else's sin lead you into sin. Taking the high road of encouragement is more difficult, but it also yields much better relationship results. These practical suggestions will help with any difficult relationship:

- Compile a list of all the positive traits of the other person. Start looking for what he/she is doing right, *not* what they are doing wrong. *"If you search for good, you will find favor; but if you search for evil, it will find you"* (Proverbs 11:27). No one is perfect, but sometimes we have to dig deep to find the good. Of course, usually I'm digging through my own baggage, like unreasonable expectations. Let's be women who encourage the people in our lives to become all God created them to be!

- Tell the other person what you appreciate about them.
- Compliment them in front of others.
- Say "thank you."
- Join them in one of their hobbies.
- Absolutely pray over them. My mother once gave me a prayer she would pray over my father. It would start with his head and end at his feet. Yes, I have an awesome mom. Although she prayed this over my father, we can pray it over anyone in our lives. Over the years I have put my own spin on it. Here's my Cliffs Notes version:

I pray for clarity of mind and thought today for (insert name).
I also pray for:

> *Nothing unholy to be set before his/her eyes*
>
> *Eyes to look with compassion upon a hurting world*
>
> *A mouth that speaks words of life and encourages those he/she comes in contact with today*
>
> *A heart that loves You first and foremost, beating in time with our Savior's*
>
> *The work of his/her hands to be blessed*
>
> *Guidance for his/her steps, so he/she is always walking in your will*

If we struggle with having a critical spirit, we need to repent and ask God to help us overcome this inclination. We can change. The girlfriend I mentioned earlier who was prone to criticizing her husband is proof of this. It has not been easy for her, but with the Lord's help she has learned to push "pause" on her words before they leave her mouth. She is focusing on what her husband does right, and their marriage is blossoming because of it. This can be our story too.

It is a *Time to Build Up*. Build up our family. Build up our friends. Build up those God puts in our path. When we do, we will find the blessings come back tenfold.

Make It Personal

1. How have others come alongside you to build you up?

2. What can you do today to build up someone?

3. Do you struggle with a critical spirit? If so, repent and ask for God's help to overcome.

4

A Time to Cry

I once visited a woman who lived in an old neighborhood surrounded by large trees. She told me a story of being awakened one night by the cry of a baby outside. Disturbed, she went out to check. It took a while for her to find where the cry was coming from, but eventually she looked up in a tree and saw an eagle. He was crying.

Eagles are one of the few animals in nature that mate for life. This particular eagle had been one of two living in the tree. Alone now, it cried every night for weeks until, one day, the woman noticed the eagle with a new mate. She never heard the mournful cry again.

I'm not a crier. It's not that I don't cry...it's just that it takes a lot for me to get to that point. Most of my girlfriends can tear up pretty easily and frequently, but not me. When I do finally cry, it usually begins innocently enough and quickly cascades into ugly, uncontrollable sobbing. My theory is that my body sees its opportunity to release some stress and unleashes my storehouse of unshed tears.

I mentioned earlier that I suffered from a type of PTSD, which disconnected me from my feelings to a large degree. This impacted my ability to embrace the feelings, such as sadness and grief, which can lead to tears. I was an expert at shutting down sad feelings. Although on the surface, this might be preferable, it also prevents a person from processing the pain. Once I admitted that my past was negatively affecting my present and, left alone, would impact my future, I accepted that I needed to change. One of the indicators that my therapy was working was when I was able to cry, which was proof of my ability to feel a range of emotions again.

I learned how to cry over some of the painful events in my past. When I was an eight-year-old little girl, a neighbor sexually abused me. I felt confused, powerless and ashamed. Abuse is difficult for an adult to understand, and nearly impossible for a child. As a young girl, I was forced to make an adult-level decision about what to do. Unfortunately, I didn't tell my parents, which left me open to future abuse.

My little girl logic was that I didn't want to make my parents sad, and I innately knew this would make them sad. In fact, after a while, the memories faded. Some may be shocked to think anyone could truly push such events from their mind, but I've always called it my Scarlett O'Hara-ness. "I can't think about that now...I'll just think about that tomorrow. Tomorrow is another day."

I easily forget things I actually want to remember, so it doesn't surprise me that I can forget what I want to forget. I possess a remarkable ability to forget not only the mundane, but also the bigger life-impacting events as well. It's really remarkable—not because it's a skill worthy of the *Guinness Book of World Records*, mind you, but because it happens so frequently. I will always need my best friend, because she remembers my life so much better than I do. Big gaps in memory are fairly common with PTSD sufferers. Honestly, it could be seen as a gift, considering that I was happy to forget a lot of things. It took a while to realize that forgetting intellectually doesn't mean forgetting emotionally. The pain and the hurt were still present, manipulating my interpretation of life and influencing my decisions, only I didn't understand the *why* behind some of the choices I made.

My memory of the sexual abuse all came rushing back years later when I ran into my abuser. I remembered, but still didn't tell anyone or shed a tear. Since PTSD can be triggered by one traumatic event or a series of them, I came to realize that the ability to close off my sad feelings could be traced all the way back to my eight-year-old response to the sexual abuse. Unfortunately, I took those learned coping skills of turning off my emotions and later honed them to perfection in an unhealthy marriage.

I felt confused, powerless, and ashamed.

The first time I told anyone about my childhood abuse I was in my mid-twenties and going through the adoption process for my oldest daughter, Jerilyn. A social worker came to do a home study and asked a ton of questions. One of those questions was whether either of us had ever been sexually abused.

I admitted I had, but immediately followed up by telling her it hadn't affected me in my life, so there was no need to be concerned. Yes, this is actually what I told a social worker, and the scary part is, I totally meant it. She gave me a very strange look and made me promise to seek counseling about it. I did promise her, although it took me about ten years to fulfill the promise.

Eighteen years after the abuse, plus a few months of therapy, I cried for the first time about it. I cried for my lost innocence and the ripple effect of damage. I forgave myself for choosing not to tell anyone and let go of the responsibility I felt—placing the responsibility back on the shoulders of the actual perpetrator. He made a choice. I lived with it the best way my little girl mind would let me.

I have shared my story as God leads me and have been shocked at how many women have confided they carry around a similar secret themselves. My heart breaks for each woman, and I am positive that God's does as well. If you have your own story, let me encourage you to tell someone and seek help (see Appendix A)…maybe sooner than the eighteen years it took me. Satan loves for us to keep our hurts in the dark, but once we shine the light on those injuries, healing can begin.

DIVORCE

I never thought I'd be divorced. No one ever does. Yet, divorce is happening at an alarming rate in our country. We all know someone close to us affected by divorce; it may even be your story. I wonder how many tears have fallen over broken promises and broken marriages. We won't ever know, but God knows.

> You keep track of all my sorrows. You have collected all my tears in your bottle. You have recorded each one in your book (Psalm 56:8).

Our pain is relevant to God. He cares. After nine years, my marriage was struggling to survive. Even with the difficulties we were experiencing, I believed and prayed God would perform a miracle, turning everything around. Then, in one day, my whole world came crashing down.

Someone I knew extremely well approached me and revealed my husband's unfaithfulness. My first reaction was disbelief. Unfortunately, it only took a minute for me to start putting pieces together. Then came the nausea and the tears.

The next few days were a blur as I confronted him, asked him to leave, and begged God for discernment. My husband was denying everything and accusing this woman of lying. Since they both had a long history of lying, I honestly didn't know what to believe. After asking them both to take a lie detector test, she agreed and my husband refused.

I went to bed that night asking God for evidence, and He woke me with an idea on how to obtain proof. It was obvious the idea was from God, since it was five o'clock in the morning, and my brain doesn't start to truly function for the day until about noon. As a late night girl, mornings are not my favorite. In fact, I'm hopeful there won't even be mornings in heaven!

This day though, I was wide-awake and grateful to God for the idea. A verse kept running through my mind: *"Though He slay me, yet will I trust*

Him" (Job 13:15, KJV). I felt slayed, but consciously decided to trust God. I pulled out a book of worship songs and started singing praises to God. Thirty minutes into sweet fellowship with the Lord, I reached for my Bible and prayed, *Lord, I **need** You to speak to me. I don't know who to believe.*

I opened my Bible, trusting God would speak to me through His Word. My Bible opened to Psalm 55.

> *Listen to my prayer, O God. Do not ignore my cry for help! Please listen and answer me, for I am overwhelmed by my troubles. My enemies shout at me, making loud and wicked threats. They bring trouble on me and angrily hunt me down. My heart pounds in my chest. The terror of death assaults me. Fear and trembling overwhelm me, and I can't stop shaking. Oh, that I had wings like a dove; then I would fly away and rest! I would fly far away to the quiet of the wilderness. How quickly I would escape—far from this wild storm of hatred.*
>
> *Confuse them, Lord, and frustrate their plans, for I see violence and conflict in the city. Its walls are patrolled day and night against invaders, but the real danger is wickedness within the city. Everything is falling apart; threats and cheating are rampant in the streets (Psalm 55: 1-11).*

Up to this point, I related entirely to the Psalm. I was shaking, afraid and wanted to escape. After the last stanza, I broke down and the tears flowed. "In the city" correlated to "in my marriage." My husband had threatened me. Cheating was "rampant." I felt like I knew at this point, but felt compelled to read on through my tears. The Psalm became even more poignant.

> *It is not an enemy who taunts me—I could bear that. It is not my foes who so arrogantly insult me—I could have hidden from them. Instead, it is you—my equal, my companion and*

close friend. What good fellowship we once enjoyed as we walked together to the house of God (Psalm 55:12-14).

Then, as if this passage wasn't confirmation enough, God's Word continued to drive the message home for me.

For my enemies refuse to change their ways; they do not fear God. As for my companion, he betrayed his friends; he broke his promises. His words are as smooth as butter, but in his heart is war. His words are as soothing as lotion, but underneath are daggers (Psalm 55:19b-21).

God spoke to me clearly through His Word and ample evidence was found later that confirmed what God had revealed to me. God's Word is true. He uses it to speak truth into our lives. I've read the entire Bible many times and have camped out in the Psalms for long stretches. Yet, at that moment, I needed this *exact* chapter; nothing else would have been as clear. I felt God release me from my marriage the moment I finished reading the chapter.

This is my story. We all have our own stories. I often say that the safest place to be is in the center of God's will, and sometimes God's will takes us to very difficult places. God made it clear I was to pursue a divorce; but for others, their path may be to stay and forgive. God is in the business of restoring marriages and showing us the healing power of forgiveness. The most important thing is to be in an intimate relationship with the Lord so we can hear His still, small voice guiding us.

CRYING OUT TO GOD

During my divorce and the difficult year following it, I found it very challenging to pray. I could read the Bible, go to church, even teach Bible studies, but praying remained entirely different. When praying, my pain was laid bare. There was no hiding behind a smile, or a quick answer to the question, "How are you doing?" God knew the truth. There were no pretenses with Him. He knew the pain and the deep level of hurt.

God witnessed the tears no one else saw. Let me encourage you to go to God with your pain. Don't run from Him. He is the best physician, psychologist and counselor...and He knows what you need even better than you do. Cry with Him, and let the healing begin.

Make It Personal

1. If you have ever been the victim of sexual abuse, promise God you will talk about it with someone… a friend, family member or counselor.

2. What do you need to cry out to God about?

3. Can you think of a time God has used His Word to speak truth into your life? If you can't, ask God to give you that gift and start reading His Word daily.

5

A Time to Dance

I love to dance. Growing up in a Southern Baptist church, I was not *supposed* to love to dance….actually, I'm not even *supposed* to know *how* to dance! Shhh….it will be our little secret!

I love watching professional ballroom dancers out on the floor. It is amazing how fluid they appear. The dancers seem to float across the floor effortlessly. They make it look so easy, but everyone knows it takes a lot of hard work, time and effort to be able to produce such a beautiful partnership. I find myself comparing that beautiful partnership to the one I am endeavoring to develop between God and myself. I call it my dance of faith.

I remember what it felt like going to my first dance, nervously hoping I would not be left standing on the sidelines, and secretly dreaming the cutest boy in my class would ask me out onto the floor. I also recall how totally out of my control it felt. Not being brave enough to ask a boy to dance left me at the mercy of whether the boys chose me for a dance partner or not.

However, in the dance of faith, my partner is God. The wonderful thing about God being my partner is that my dance card will always be full. God has written Himself down on every line. He doesn't just want me for one dance. He wants to be my permanent partner. He has eyes only for me (or, in your case, *you*). God created women with a need to be cherished, and God doesn't create a need that He Himself cannot fill. He chooses us, and He cherishes us.

I am confronted on a daily basis with opportunities to exercise my faith. It is fairly easy to enter into the dance of faith when God is asking me to do something I am already comfortable doing. Other times, it is difficult to begin the dance, because God is asking me to try something new that I know will challenge me.

Regardless of what God asks me to step out in faith and do, I find myself at the dance. My partner has asked me to join Him on the floor, but the catch is that I need to actually decide to leave the sidelines and dance. He is a perfect gentleman, waiting on me, no matter how long it takes. The problem is, some of us are really comfortable on the sidelines in our faith. We know God is asking us to step out, but while our spirit may be willing, our flesh is still weak.

We sit on the sidelines because we are afraid to dance.

Afraid of change.

Afraid to submit to God's lead.

Afraid of what others will think.

Afraid we will fail.

I am raising three daughters, and one of the first verses I had them memorize was, *"For God has not given us a spirit of fear, but of power and of love and of a sound mind"* (2 Timothy 1:7, NKJV). My girls are always giving me opportunities to exercise my faith muscles. Sometimes it is in the small things, like praying God will help us find something we have lost. This prayer is most often for my own scattered possessions! Now my children are the ones to remind me that we should stop and pray. He's answered before…why wouldn't He answer again? One of my daughters prays for green lights when we are running late, which is often, and we miraculously start hitting green lights. I believe God is using the small things to build my children's faith. We all have a dance to do, regardless of age.

SAY NO TO FEAR AND YES TO FAITH

Although God does ask me to trust Him in the small things, He also asks me to step out in faith on the big, scary things too. The first time I had to go in front of a judge required a huge amount of faith. It was not long after my separation, and I was on my first of what would end up being many lawyers.

God created women with a need to be cherished, and God doesn't create a need that He Himself cannot fill. He chooses us, and He cherishes us.

Although my husband and I had adopted our oldest daughter, he never treated her the same as our two biological children. I felt the Holy Spirit telling me very strongly that Jerilyn should not be in his care. When I explained the situation to my lawyer, she told me no judge would consider her custody and visitation separately from our other daughters. Moments before walking into the courtroom, I was standing in the hallway, fighting with my lawyer in order to convince her to even request this from the judge. She finally agreed, but warned me that it was extremely unlikely that the judge would agree.

When uncomfortable in a situation, I used to wear a mask—usually without even realizing it. My mask was a smile. The more uncomfortable I was, the harder it was to get the mask to come off.

Going into a courtroom for the first time made me extremely uncomfortable. I think courtrooms are designed to be intimidating with their raised bench for the judge, armed bailiff, dark walls, extreme silence and freezing temperatures. My hands were shaking so hard I had to hide them under the desk. My prayer before going in was that God would remove the mask and let the judge see my real feelings.

When it came time for my lawyer to bring up separating out Jerilyn, I could see her hesitation. After she made the request, the judge stopped everything and looked directly at me for at least twenty seconds. There was total silence in the courtroom. After twenty seconds, which felt like twenty minutes, he said to me, "I can tell, just by the look on your face, how serious this matter is, and I am going to grant your request."

My lawyer's mouth dropped open. All I could think was *Thank You, God!* Not only did He answer my prayer request, He even had the judge comment directly on the fact that my real feelings were not hidden behind a mask. Our God is so good! He had asked me to fight a battle, in faith I did, and He showed His miraculous power.

When I say no to fear and yes to faith, it's amazing what happens. God asks me to take a first step in faith, and as soon as I do, all of a sudden I realize it wasn't as hard as I thought it would be. I am infused with strength and hope. Why do we let fear hold us back from the wonderful experiences God has planned for us?

Once we take the first step, our dance with God can begin. He reaches His hand out to us and we grab hold. Step by step, we are taught by the perfect teacher.

His love endures forever. (Even if we step on His toes a time or two!)

His patience never runs out.

His encouragement makes us feel safe.

His faithful character is worthy of our trust.

Before we know it, we will be floating across the floor as effortlessly as those professional ballroom dancers. Those beautiful dances didn't start out smoothly for them, and it won't for us either. However, the more we dance, the easier it becomes. Pretty soon, you will look like a professional. Only you and God will know when you miss a step. You will learn how to recover quickly and keep dancing.

Don't we want a testimony of faith that encourages others to step out from the sidelines? I do. I want people to see me dance with my Lord and bring glory to Him. I can just hear the crowd now... *"If He can make that clumsy girl look like she knows what she's doing, He deserves some glory!"* It's true, if He can take this girl off the sidelines and teach her to love the dance,

He can and will do the same for any one of us.

Regardless of what we are facing in life right now, whether things are peachy keen or we feel like there is no light at the end of the tunnel, God is patiently waiting for us. If we listen carefully, I think we will hear, "Precious daughter, May I have this dance?"

Make It Personal

1. What is God asking you to step out in faith and do?

2. When was the last time you said no to fear and yes to faith?

3. What is an example in your life, or in the life of someone you know, where God has showed up miraculously?

6

A Time to Die

My wonderful friend, Candy, went to be with the Lord at far too young an age. She was raising four amazing children; her illness and subsequent death came as a complete shock to everyone. Candy was my neighbor in Selah, Washington. Selah is a tiny town in eastern Washington, right outside of Yakima. I'm a big city girl myself, so it was quite an adjustment for me to live there. One friend made life bearable—Candy. We immediately connected and began spending a lot of time together.

When I was pregnant with my first child, Ainsley, Candy and I walked together early each morning. She was one of those women who had a gift for parenting, and I wanted to soak up as much wisdom from her as possible. Her family welcomed us and invited us to spend holidays with them.

Once Ainsley was born, I quickly discovered colic was an honest to God, real thing. She was not a happy camper most of the time, and I was usually alone with her, since my then husband had taken another job transfer not long after she was born. He was in another city while I rocked and rocked and rocked Ainsley day and night. She wouldn't take a pacifier or suck her thumb; the only thing that would calm her down was to suck on my finger, at a ridiculous angle.

My only reprieve was Candy and her family. Her youngest daughters would come over every day after school and hold Ainsley. I literally cried tears of joy some days when those two little girls walked in the door. I loved them so much!

I was so sad when we moved away after only a year. I missed Candy and her family, but thankfully we were able to stay in touch. I ended up sending her Rick Warren's book, *The Purpose Driven Life,* and Candy called me frequently with questions. The Holy Spirit was doing a work in her and drawing her close to Him. She had an excitement about her faith that I had not seen before. It was a precious time in our friendship. Little did we know, God would be calling her home soon after she found her way back to Him. Even in the midst of death, our God is gracious. He drew Candy to Himself and, by doing so, comforted my heart by knowing exactly where my friend went when she left this earth.

Candy passed away while I was pregnant with my next child. I loved my friend and her beautiful daughters, Daisy and Samantha Marie. I wanted to honor them when I chose my daughter's name, thus, Daisy Marie.

BE STRONG AND COURAGEOUS

Another friend of mine, Aarin, passed away after battling cancer for nearly a decade. She was in her late thirties with two young daughters. One of my favorite memories is of her smile as she discovered all of the ladies in our Bible study wearing blue nail polish in support of her battle. We loved her dearly. Although we prayed for a different ending, she continued to be an inspiration to all around her as her faith held firm even when her body failed. She compels me to wonder if I could face death with such strength and courage. The Lord told Joshua over and over again, *"Be strong and courageous"* (Joshua 1:6-9). That command makes me think of Aarin. It is possible to be strong and courageous even while fighting such a formidable opponent as death.

The death of a close friend is painful and can leave us with more questions than answers about God and His timing. The sad truth is, we all have an appointed time to leave this earth. None of us is promised tomorrow; death is inevitable. The only question is whether we are ready for it.

SPIRITUAL DEATH

Physical death is all around us, but there are other types of death as well. Spiritual death is just as real, even if we can't see or touch it and should break our hearts as much, if not more, than a physical death because of its finality. Spiritual death is when we make a choice against submitting to Christ.

> *Yes, they knew God, but they wouldn't worship him as God or even give him thanks. And they began to think up foolish ideas of what God was like. As a result, their minds became dark and confused...Since they thought it foolish to acknowledge God, he abandoned them to their foolish thinking and let them do things that should never be done. Their lives became full of every kind of wickedness...They know God's justice requires that those who do these things deserve to die, yet they do them anyway. Worse yet, they encourage others to do them, too (Romans 1:21-32).*

The inclination of our hearts being bent towards sin and not wanting to accept God's way is not something you find only outside the church. It is just as prevalent in the church. Our family used to move a lot, which inevitably led to a lot of church shopping in new cities. I've been in churches that are spiritually dead and noticed a few similarities.

The lack of joy and fellowship

No sharing of what God has done in lives recently

Worship music falling on deaf ears

Limited ministries

When we don't sense the Holy Spirit breathing life into a church, we can feel something is missing. If we attend a church where we are not being fed, and we see no growth in those around us, it may be time to evaluate the church's spiritual health. I'm not implying we need to leave the church. We may be the one God uses to bring back the spark. The key is that we will have to feed ourselves spiritually, so we can pour out God's Spirit to others.

In order to see spiritual death for what it is, we first must have a living relationship with the Lord. Then we will be able to tell the difference. The world is full of spiritual darkness, but once we experience the Holy Spirit working in our life, we don't forget it.

I remember having a conversation with my former husband, asking him when he had felt the Holy Spirit use him. At first, he didn't even understand the question. I tried to clarify it more, only to see him staring blankly back at me. I reminded him of times I thought the Holy Spirit had used him, but he remembered none of them. It was in that moment I realized I might not actually be married to a Christian, and it was a shocking revelation for me. Looking back, I can see signs all over the place, but I never thought to look for them. I was living under my safe assumption of his claim to be a Christian.

When we met, he was in the Navy and wasn't attending church. I found that easy to overlook, because he lived on a ship. Once he knew how important my faith was to me, he quickly began attending again. I say again because he grew up as a pastor's kid. He knew the role, and he knew how to play it. I was caught hook, line and sinker.

After I spent many years of our marriage hoping he would take the spiritual lead, I came to a dead end the night I realized I could never expect leadership from a man who had never personally submitted to Christ. Sometimes those who are spiritually dead are so busy going through the motions, you would never suspect their relationship with Christ is only a facade.

DIE TO SELF

Although physical and spiritual deaths are permanent, followers of God are also asked to die to self. The term "die to self" is not common outside of Christian circles, so let me explain. Dying to self is when our flesh, or sinful nature, wants to do one thing, while the spirit is telling us to do something else. We have to make a choice to either give in to our selfish desires or be obedient to God.

I am presented daily with opportunities to die to selfishness—beginning when my alarm clock goes off and I really want to hit snooze ten times, all the way to the end of the day when I am ready to veg out, but my child still needs my patient help with homework.

Dying to self requires sacrifice. It requires letting go of pride or whatever we place between God and ourselves. Early on in my separation from my former husband, he was coming back into our home on his weekend visitations until he had a more permanent living situation set up. His visits consisted of drinking and watching sports on the television, not in spending time with the girls or attempting to meet their increased emotional needs with all the recent changes.

Dying to self doesn't feel good in the moment, but it allows us to identify with Christ.

One Sunday morning, while he sat watching sports, I asked him if I could take the girls to church with me, he responded with a quick refusal because it was *his* weekend. I calmly replied, "Okay" and left to go get ready for church. A few minutes later, I heard a knock on my bedroom door. I opened it to find him glaring at me. "If you want to take the girls to church, you have to ask me *nicely*." I stood there, knowing his goal was to pick a fight, and feeling the fight or flight response rising up in me. Should I fight back or shrink away without responding? Or was there another option?

My flesh wanted to fight back. However, I knew my children would be safer with me and not alone with him. So, I swallowed my pride and took a calming breath before asking him *nicely* if I could take the girls to church. He snarled, "Fine" and stomped away because he didn't get the reaction he was hoping for.

Dying to self doesn't *feel* good in the moment, but it allows us to identify with Christ. Jesus died a violent death on the cross for us. It's our turn to die to our sinful desires for Him. Jesus tells us we are to pick up our cross daily and follow Him (Luke 9:23). Some days are easier than others. Some crosses are easier to bear, some more difficult. Your cross today may come in the form of...

Saying NO to the most popular TV show because it dishonors God

Saying YES to attending church consistently

Volunteering your time, energy or money

Apologizing for your part in an argument

Swallowing your pride and asking *nicely*

I am all too aware of the need to die to self daily if I truly want to live the blessed and abundant life God has for me. Although I do believe it gets easier over time, we still wake up every day with a decision to make. Am I going to say no to myself and yes to God today? I'll let you in on the situations where I find it most difficult.

Not letting my frustration at my children boil over

Returning evil with good

Pausing long enough to contemplate how I am going to say something, so I don't sound like a bossy brat

These are just a few examples, but believe me, there are many more where these came from! God, in His infinite love, meets us where we are and loves us enough to keep chipping away at the pieces that are not Christ-like. The experience of repenting of our sins, turning away from them and doing the right thing the next time will provide evidence the Holy Spirit is living in us. The end result of our obedience is that others will see in us a resemblance to Christ.

The earth is full of people all around us who are dying physically and spiritually, suffocated by their fear of death. It's our job to show them what Jesus looks like, how He loves, and what a great hope we have. We can and we will, by making it less about us and more about Him. *"He must become greater; I must become less"* (John 3:30, NIV).

Make It Personal

1. Whose physical death has had the most profound effect on you? In what ways do you want to be similar to them? In what ways do you want to be different?

2. When was the last time you felt the Holy Spirit working through you? If you can't remember, why can't you remember? Tell Him you are ready and willing to be used by Him.

3. In what areas do you struggle with dying to self? Think back to an experience you've had where you were obedient to God by sacrificing your desires; how did walking in obedience make you feel?

7

A Time to Embrace

In Luke 15, Jesus describes the parable of the prodigal son whose father runs to embrace him when he returns home. Although this is a poignant example of the embrace our Father has for us, when contemplating A Time to Embrace, another lesser known account in the Bible came to mind: Jacob's return to Canaan and Esau's embrace.

Jacob and Esau were twins. Jacob was the favorite of his mother, Rachel. Esau was the favorite of his father, Isaac. Jacob's name meant deceiver, and he lived up to it during his youth. First, he tricked Esau out of his birthright. Then, when Isaac was blind and on his deathbed, Rachel helped Jacob steal Esau's blessing as the firstborn. Afterwards, Jacob fled the area to avoid bloodshed…his own.

Fast-forward twenty years. Remember, no cell phones or Facebook…no way to know if Esau was still bent on revenge. Jacob sends messengers ahead to inform Esau he is moving back to town. His messengers return and report that Esau is on his way to meet Jacob with an army of 400 men. Jacob decides he'd rather be safe than sorry and begins sending gifts to hopefully soften his brother's heart before they intersect.

Jacob was frightened enough to pray, *"O LORD, please rescue me from the hand of my brother Esau. I am afraid that he is coming to attack me, along with my wives and children"* (Genesis 32:11).

However, Esau surprised Jacob. *"Then Esau ran to meet him and embraced him, threw his arms around his neck, and kissed him. And they both wept"* (Genesis 33:4). Talk about some happy tears, right? Jacob must have been thinking, *I thought my brother was going to murder us and, instead, we are rejoicing together...this could only be God.*

Some embraces are sweeter than others, aren't they?

Hugging our newborn.

First hug from our first love.

Goodbye hug before leaving.

Welcome hug upon return.

The hug through tears, when words just won't do.

I personally love it when my daughters come in after their day at school and find me wherever I am to embrace me. We all need a hug every now and then. Thankfully, God is more than willing to provide for our needs. He assures us, *"Even if my father and mother abandon me, the LORD will hold me close"* (Psalm 27:11).

An embrace can be offered as a greeting, or to convey a deeper sentiment of love, friendship, forgiveness, compassion, peace or support, to name a few. One miraculous time in my life, kneeling at the altar, pouring my heart out to God, I felt a hand of support on my shoulder calming my fears. However, when I turned around, I found no one there, at least not physically. Our God is a miraculous God.

No less miraculous have been times when I felt desperate for a touch from God and amazingly a friend showed up unexpectedly. Those friends became God's arms for me to collapse into. God will do whatever necessary to embrace us. He loves us...I mean truly, unconditionally loves us.

NOT AN ISLAND

No man or woman is an island. I learned the hard way that we all need each other. I've always had an independent streak. I started working as young as I could, babysitting full-time through the summers to buy those coveted name brand jeans and earn the right to have a car. In my family, you didn't need a car unless you had a job, so I needed a job! My parents instilled responsibility into me, which I appreciate to this day. They taught me, by example, anything worth having is worth working for. Unfortunately, I also cashed in on the other side of that independence coin—the one where you think you can do everything all on your own.

My independent outlook worked really well until I hit a place in life where I couldn't do it all on my own. We all come to that place at some point.

A prodigal child...

The loss of a job...

Separation or divorce...

A deployed spouse...

A bad report from the doctor...

The death of a loved one.

None of us walks this earth unscathed. We all face trials and, regardless of circumstances, the impact can be severe. It can affect our ability to get our own butt out of bed in the morning. Mostly, it can affect how we view God. That's when the rubber really hits the road for our faith.

It's easy to love God when life is going well, but what about when your world is falling apart? Do we love God when we don't get our way? Sometimes, before we can even address those questions, our physical needs demand our attention and feel insurmountable. On some of my first daunting days as a single mom, I remember wondering how I was going to get out of bed or take care of my children that day.

Thankfully, God showed up, whether or not I was even ready to see that it was Him. He showed up...

…in the neighbor who popped over with a meal for my family,

…in the friend who called me at just the right time,

…in the song on the radio reminding me to keep my focus on God,

…or in a passage from God's Word that spoke directly to my heart.

It always amazes me. God doesn't just say, "Hey, buck up! Do you think you are the first person to experience this?" No…God sits down with us. He is filled with compassion for us. As he sits with us, healing our brokenness, He lovingly leads others to come alongside us and meet our physical needs.

In my darkest days, God met the needs of my children and me through others. Some were family, some were good friends, some were neighbors (who then became good friends), and some were almost complete strangers to me. I stopped being Ms. Independent and embraced the idea of letting others minister to me. I developed deeper relationships and a better understanding of God's character by admitting my brokenness and asking for help, without shame, from those around me. In fact, I've probably gotten too good at it. I'm pretty sure my neighbors and friends wish I wouldn't ask for any more!

I developed deeper relationships and a better understanding of God's character by admitting my brokenness.

We all have seasons in our lives. During some, our cups are overflowing with ministry opportunities God has placed in front of us. But in other seasons, we need to be on the receiving end of that type of ministry. These seasons of need are a time to embrace new ways of viewing our role in this world, whether we start out as Ms. Independent or not.

EMBRACE THE TOUGH STUFF

An embrace can also be an acceptance of a new reality. Life isn't all a bed of roses, at least for me, and I'm willing to bet it isn't for any one of us. I have had my fair share of unpredicted storms. Meteorologists seem to have the ability to inaccurately predict the weather, and yet their failure to predict rarely impacts them. I wish my life were similar. Unfortunately, it seems my unpredicted storms definitely have an impact by making my life more challenging.

When we adopted my oldest daughter, I surely didn't anticipate I would later discover she was autistic and bi-polar or that I would one day be a single mom raising three girls. Although we can't anticipate most of the challenges we face, if we are to learn from them, we must embrace them. If we don't, we find ourselves fighting reality.

When Jerilyn was first evaluated, I didn't want to *label* her because I thought it would place limitations on her. Honestly, I didn't want to label myself either. I didn't want to be a "special needs mom." After realizing having the formal diagnosis was what got her the services she desperately needed, I threw away my pride and accepted the fact that my daughter has special needs. If I hadn't been able to do that, she wouldn't have access to the services and education she needs to be successful.

Ignoring reality rarely works. Sometimes it is something in others, but more often it is a reality about ourselves that we choose to ignore.

Perfectionist

Arrogant

Fearful

Controlling

Argumentative

At times, we must force ourselves to embrace a truth we would rather avoid. It is a measure of emotional intelligence to be willing to examine yourself and see areas that need improvement. We don't have to stay where we are today. We can change, but it starts with accepting the truth.

If we can't think of any areas for improvement, we need to ask those around us—I'm sure they can fill in the blank. We can't become a better version of ourselves without transforming. God says it best:

*And do not be conformed to this world, but be **transformed** by the renewing of your mind, that you may prove what the will of God is, that which is good and acceptable and perfect (Romans 12:2).*

EMBRACE THE TRANSFORMATION!

Make It Personal

1. What physical embrace was most impactful for you? Your first boyfriend, a husband being deployed or better yet returning from deployment, a parent's open arms?

2. What truth are you ignoring? About a loved one? About yourself? How can you move towards embracing it?

3. How would your life change if you did embrace that truth?

8

A Time to Gather Stones

Have you ever been asked to do something you didn't feel capable of doing?

Take on the task of Homeroom Mom

Lead a discussion group

Start a ministry

Homeschool your kiddos

Write a book

God seems to ask me to do things that leave me feeling underqualified and overwhelmed. Of course, if He asked me to do only what I'm *over*confident about, I wouldn't have to grow my faith. Instead, God has so *graciously* given me opportunity after opportunity to move to deeper places with Him through divorce, single parenting, foster parenting, poverty, special needs children and courtroom battles to name a few. Sure, I sometimes feel like I'm drowning in deep water, but He has kept me afloat every time, evidenced by the fact that I am writing this and not rocking in a corner. You may be facing some unexpected situations of your own that don't feel at all like opportunities, but don't despair. God has always been in the business of building the faith of His beloved ones.

I imagine Joshua felt underqualified and overwhelmed with the role God gave him of leading an estimated two to three million Israelites into the Promised Land. One of the first challenges he had as their leader was guiding them across the Jordan River.

The Israelites, with Joshua at the helm, came upon the rushing Jordan River overflowing its banks. After forty years of wandering in the desert, the time had finally come to cross over into the Promised Land. As the feet of the priests carrying the Ark of the Covenant hit the water, the water stopped flowing and the riverbed began drying out. I wonder how it must have felt to be one of those priests. They courageously stepped into a raging river carrying precious cargo. The river dried up more with each step of faith they took. As the priests stood in the middle of the riverbed, on dry ground, the whole nation of Israel crossed the Jordan.

Joshua commanded twelve men, one from each tribe, to pick up a stone from the very place the priests were standing. They gathered the stones together for a memorial. *"These stones will stand as a memorial among the people of Israel forever"* (Joshua 4:7).

Can you imagine the emotion of the whole nation on that day? They had spent a lifetime waiting to cross over the Jordan into a land flowing with milk and honey. I say *lifetime* because as a consequence for their sins, the first generation of Israelites passed away before entering the Promised Land. Those left were the children of the older generation. What a poignant moment to create a memorial.

In the hearts of the people, these stones not only symbolized the miracle they participated in by crossing the Jordan River on dry ground, but also a remembrance of all those loved ones who weren't able to make it across. How fitting that God ushered the Israelites into the desert with the parting of the Red Sea and then brought them full circle as He parted the waters once again to bring them out.

I always like to bring home a souvenir from each vacation to help me remember something unique about the experience. One of my favorite mementos is a silver tea set I purchased on a trip to Istanbul, Turkey. Whenever I see it, I remember the sights and sounds of shopping among the 3,000 shops at The Grand Bazaar. This habit of mine makes me wonder if any of the Israelites picked up a small stone from the riverbed as a remembrance of the miracle God performed.

REMEMBERING TOGETHER

Ironically, I am writing this chapter on the anniversary of the September 11 terrorist attacks on our country. I didn't plan for this chapter to coincide with this particular date when I began the book, but I do see it as an example of God's perfect timing. Spending much of my day watching clips reminded me of both the tragic and heroic events of that day.

I watched as the friends and family of the victims stood together around the 9/11 Memorial, reverently touching the names of their loved ones etched in bronze. The memorial's twin reflecting pools are nearly an acre each in size and feature the largest manmade waterfalls in North America. The two pools sit within the footprints of where the Twin Towers once stood.

Memorials help us to remember and dare us never to forget. We gather together around them to express solidarity and share in life's tragedies and triumphs. When difficulties arise, we come alongside one another and help shoulder the burdens.

BE A GATHERER

In Jacksonville, Florida, my neighbors were a godsend who not only helped me shoulder the burdens, but also taught me the value of friendship. We could often be found chatting outside as the children played and afternoon turned into dusk. One day, I walked over to the house of a neighbor none of us had really gotten to know yet. I was determined to get her outside and force her to waste, I mean spend, time with us.

The exchange went something like this:

Me: (knock, knock)

Her: (door opens slowly) Hi. (uttered with definite trepidation)

Me: Hey! Do you want to come outside for a little while *[to play]*?

Her: Thanks, but I can't. My house is a mess, and I really need to clean.

Me: Oh, c'mon. That can wait *[like it is doing right now at my house]*.

Her: No, I really need to get this done. (Code for "No, I'm an introvert and just want to be left alone.")

Me: Okay, well how about I help you clean so you can come join us outside?

Her: (Speechless…most likely thinking, "I'm not even sure how to respond to this almost perfect stranger who is offering to come inside my home and clean it.")

Me: (Walking in uninvited) So, where do we start?

Her: Ummm…

Me: How about I clean up the kitchen?

Her: (Resigned to losing the battle with the crazy, bossy lady now in her kitchen.) Okay.

Fast-forward thirty minutes, and we were bonded by bleach. She came out to "play" with the rest of us and ended up never trying to bow out again. My hesitant neighbor became one of my closest friends. We still laugh about the impromptu cleaning party I hosted in her messy house.

My motto: Cleaning stinks…
but it stinks less when you do it with friends.

I'm not suggesting everyone needs to go and force your way into a neighbor's home. I can see the same scenario, which played out fine for us, going terribly wrong and ending with the calling of police and cementing a neighbor equals enemy situation. So, please, no letters asking for my advice when and if you are charged with breaking, entering and cleaning.

We don't have to wait for a ray of light to shine down and the sound of angels singing before we gather around a friend. I'm sure if we pause for a moment to think of the women we know, we can easily come up with one who could use a little encouragement or a helping hand. Why not reach out to her?

Make a double batch of dinner tonight and take her family a meal.

Watch her kids so she and her husband can go on a date.

Schedule a manicure for the two of you—and you treat.

Or my favorite, of course—surprise her with an impromptu cleaning party!

At some times in our lives, we need to gather around a friend; at other times, we are the one in need of some support. I consider myself blessed by the friends who lifted me up in my darkest moments. They were my rocks, offering solid, sound biblical advice and soft, sensitive arms to hold me. Let me encourage each one of us to be that safe place for someone else.

Gather friends by being one first.

Make It Personal

1. What have you been asked to do that you didn't feel capable of doing?

2. Have you ever visited a memorial that really impacted you?

3. Who do you know that could use a helping hand? Spend a few minutes in prayer asking God how to best help that person.

9

A Time to Grieve

Grief is defined as feeling deep sorrow. Grieving over someone or something is one of the deepest emotions we experience as humans and can leave us changed forever. It can alter the way we view life and force us to face the finality of life. We can grieve the loss of people, relationships and dreams.

Some of you may have experienced the deep sorrow of the death of a child, a spouse or even a parent. I can't even imagine the pain these elicit, and I won't pretend to understand the places God has had to walk you through. My heart breaks for you and the pain you've endured.

Life will eventually teach us all about grieving the physical death of a loved one. Unfortunately, some learn that lesson earlier in life than others.

Within a one-month time period, my twenty-one-year-old cousin, David, and my grandmother both passed away. At my cousin's funeral, I watched in amazement at how my aunt, uncle and David's sister were facing the unexpected loss. The song "I Can Only Imagine" was sung by two of David's friends, and as I stood there with tears streaming down my face, I could feel the Holy Spirit's presence in the room so powerfully I had the urge to raise my hand in praise. While pondering for a brief moment if that was permissible at a funeral, I looked up and saw David's dad and sister with hands raised in praise.

Praise in the midst of the deepest grief.

Faith even in the darkest of moments.

Love for a God who gives and takes away.

Truly inspirational.

LAZARUS

John 11 tells us the story of Lazarus' death. Jesus was a good friend of Lazarus' family, which included his sisters, Mary and Martha. Jesus received the message that Lazarus was sick, but waited to return to Bethany until four days after Lazarus was buried.

Mary and Martha were grieving the loss of their brother when Jesus arrived in town. Mary, the one who loved listening to Jesus' teachings during earlier visits and who would later anoint Jesus' feet with oil, stayed at the house when she heard He was on His way, but Martha ran out to meet Him. Martha was the get-it-done sister; she didn't put off till tomorrow what could be done today. We can see this in their earlier encounter with Jesus, when she was complaining that Mary should be helping her with the hosting duties instead of putting aside her responsibilities and sitting at Jesus' feet.

When Martha met Jesus outside of the town, she said, *"Lord, if only you had been here, my brother would not have died. But even now I know that God will give you whatever you ask."* Jesus responded, *"Your brother will rise again"* (John 11: 21-23). Then they proceed to have a conversation where Jesus is clearly saying there is no limit to God's power, but Martha is not able to grasp the outside-of-the-box faith Jesus is asking of her. She is firmly grounded in reality.

Jesus then asks Martha to go get Mary. Mary immediately comes and falls at Jesus' feet. I find it interesting that all three times Mary is mentioned in the

Bible, she is at her Rabbi's feet—learning as he teaches, collapsed in her grief, or anointing him before his burial. Her words are similar to Martha's. *"Lord, if only you had been here, my brother would not have died."* However, these were her only words. Mary was the sister led by her emotions.

Mary was overcome by her grief, unable to say more, although her tears spoke loudly to her Savior's heart. When we see others in deep emotional pain, our hearts go out to them. Although fully God, Jesus was fully human as well. Jesus was "troubled" and "wept" (John 11:35). Jesus responded to Martha and Mary differently because he knew each of them intimately. He responded to Martha with a matter-of-fact answer, *"Your brother will rise again."* His response to Mary wasn't verbal—He simply wept with her.

When we cry our hearts out in grief, remember that Jesus sees our grief and feels it with us. We are not alone in it. He is our Comforter.

Perhaps we relate more to Martha's way of grieving, talking it out with friends or finding things to distract us from the deep pain so we can continue to place one foot in front of the other. God made us all differently for a reason. No one can tell anyone else how they need to grieve; we each grieve differently.

This story has an ending no one expected as Lazarus is raised from the dead. God has the ability to turn the most dire circumstances completely around. He tells Martha, *"Didn't I tell you that you would see God's glory if you believe?"* (John 11:40).

We may not see our loved one alive on earth again, but we can still see God's glory if we believe.

GRIEVING THE DEATH OF A RELATIONSHIP

The deep emotions of grief are not limited only to physical death; they can also manifest after the death of a marriage or relationship. The day I went to the courthouse to finalize my divorce, I remember feeling like I was going to a funeral. I wore black. After nine years of marriage, it took only two minutes for a judge to sever that union forever. My marriage breathed its last breath and died.

Leaving the courthouse, I couldn't believe life was still the same for everyone else. Cars still stopped at the traffic lights. People chatted while walking down the street. I wondered why everything looked the same when my world had just stopped spinning.

Our struggle is not wasted. He uses every bit of what we endure for His ultimate glory.

I am an off-the-charts extrovert, which means I like to talk...a lot. In fact, when anything big, weird, funny or significant happens, I have to tell someone before it feels real. Just ask my friend Misty, who has heard every (in)significant detail.

Uncharacteristically, the day my marriage died, I didn't want to talk to anyone. I got into my car and drove home, wanting to be alone. Even though the divorce process had taken nine months, it was hard to believe it was over. I didn't want to tell anyone, because that would make it feel too real.

I've talked with other women who expressed very similar emotions. I now recognize it as the first stage of grief, denial. When devastation hits, we are in a state of shock. Denial helps us survive the initial loss and pain. I had an intense desire to distance myself from the reality that was suffocating me. However, if healing is our goal, we must move through denial and process the pain. If we don't, we risk getting stuck there and expending all our emotional energy fighting the truth.

GRIEVING THE LOSS OF A HOME

Although, I eventually processed through the grief of my lost marriage, more losses followed. Five years after my divorce, I was in the worst financial position in my life. My former husband was behind over $30,000 in child support and alimony. Making my mortgage payments was impossible, which meant I was losing my home. With no family in Florida, I realized I was going to have to move.

After being a single mom on my own for five years, I desperately needed some family support. My family lived in Phoenix, but in order to leave the state, a judge had to grant me permission. In Florida, it is very difficult to get such permission if you are divorced and the other parent still lives in the state.

However, since our last year in Florida was extremely difficult financially, God was able to use that deficiency to help get us the approval we needed to leave the state. Living through the worst of times created the opportunity we needed in order to move.

It's easy to think God doesn't hear our prayers when we are crying out for what we perceive not as just wants, but needs, and we don't see immediate resolutions. Remember, God may be working out a much better plan than we can see at the moment. Our struggle is not wasted. He uses every bit of what we endure for His ultimate glory. We are daughters of a mighty King with everything at His disposal; if we don't see a solution right now, there is a reason. If we just keep pressing into Him, He will lead us in the right direction.

Although it was a gift that we were able to move closer to family, my heart was still in Florida. It took a few years for me to realize that I needed to grieve the loss of my home and community.

GRIEVING THE PAST

Many of us are grieving over painful events from our past. Living in this sinful, fallen world ensures we all endure difficult times. I've met women who describe childhoods filled with abuse of all kinds. So many endure the rejection of parents, and their pain is still raw.

When dwelling on these hurtful experiences, it is easy to sink into a pit of despair and depression. It is difficult to reconcile a painful past with an omnipresent and omniscient God. We are tempted to wonder, if God is there and has the power to control all things, why He would allow such hurts to happen to us.

I don't have any answers for those kinds of questions. In my own life, when I start to question why, I try to focus on what I know to be true about God...

He loves me.

He chose me.

He died for me.

He has a plan for me—to prosper me, not to harm me.

He will work all things out for my good.

I'm human, with a finite brain and limited abilities to understand myself and even the world around me. God is infinite. What I do know is that the creator of the entire universe has me in the palm of His hand. He can take the pain of my past and craft it into something of beauty. All I have to do is hand it over to Him. Everyone has a past that is unique, but not a mystery to God. Give your past to Him, and I guarantee He will bring beauty from the ashes.

> *To all who mourn in Israel, he will give a crown of beauty for ashes, a joyous blessing instead of mourning, festive praise instead of despair. In their righteousness, they will be like great oaks that the Lord has planted for his own glory (Isaiah 61:3).*

Make It Personal

1. We may not see our loved one alive on earth again, but we can still see God's glory if we believe. In what way can you imagine seeing God's glory? Think outside the box.

2. Which loss has had the most profound impact on your life?

3. What do you know to be true about God? Make a new list or add to mine. Find Scripture verses that support each truth.

10

A Time to Harvest

My daughter brought home a radish a couple of weeks ago. She was beaming with pride. Why? Because it came from the garden her class helped to cultivate at school. The fact that my daughter doesn't even like radishes didn't diminish her happiness. She had a part in the planting and harvesting.

Hard work produces results, whether you find yourself working on a…

Research paper,

DIY project,

New business endeavor, or

Cleaning the kitchen. (Disclaimer for this one…I never personally feel a sense of accomplishment when I clean my home, because within an hour, if I'm even that blessed, my work will seemingly disappear as my children create new messes. Of course, that could just be me.)

Many of these jobs take hard work, time and energy to accomplish, but once they are completed, we have some evidence of our effort. This is why scrapbooking appealed to me. I am not a super crafty person, but I was really drawn to scrapbooking for several years. With three children under five, my days were filled with tasks that had to be done and redone all over again every day. I felt that nothing lasted. At least with a scrapbook, I had something to show for my hard work.

Running after small children all day is an exhausting job. To those who are currently doing it, keep persevering. What you are doing is so very important, and eternal rewards are coming. For those of us who have already survived it, can I get a collective "Whew"? I don't know about you, but I'm counting on reaping the harvest of Proverbs 31:28, *"Her children rise up and call her blessed,"* and sooner rather than later is my preference.

SPIRITUAL HARVEST

While Jesus walked among the crowds, He saw the needs of the lost and hurting souls. Crowds have not changed. They are still filled with lost and hurting souls. Harvesters are always in demand.

> *Then he [Jesus] said to his disciples,* "The harvest is plentiful but the workers are few. Ask the Lord of the harvest, therefore, to send out workers into his harvest field" *(Matthew 9:37-38).*

Whether we grew up on a farm or not, we have all seen movies or documentaries detailing what it takes for a farmer to bring in a crop. It is an "all hands on deck" situation. One person alone cannot harvest a field; it takes a team, all working together to accomplish a common goal.

The same is true when it comes to bringing in a spiritual harvest. It doesn't happen through the efforts of only one person. As great an evangelist as Billy Graham was, he needed a team; it takes more than any one person to win the masses. Someone had to book the facility, create marketing pieces, train local church members to be counselors and complete countless other pieces of the puzzle. Only then could Billy Graham, or any other evangelist, have the opportunity to present the gift of salvation in a way that moved people to open their hearts to Jesus.

The body of Christ is full of men and women with spiritual gifts, and when working together, those gifts are the prescription to save the lost and hurting souls wandering this world. We each have an important role to play. One thing we can all do is pray for a spiritual harvest to sweep through our nation and bring a revival. Prayer is a vital part of the process.

At one time in my life I felt like I must not be doing such a great job of being a Christian, because I wasn't reaching lost souls. The real question to ask ourselves is not, "Who was the last person I led to the Lord?" Instead, it is, "Am I listening and being obedient to the Holy Spirit?"

The Bible says it is the job of the Father to draw people unto Himself (John 6:44). Harvest obedience to Him, and He will be able to use you in the ways that will bring Him the most glory.

HARVEST JOY AND HAPPINESS

You may be going through trial after trial right now and struggling to remember what living a life without constant attack feels like. Peter tells us, *"So be truly glad. There is wonderful joy ahead, even though you have to endure **many** trials for a **little** while"* (1 Peter 1:6, emphasis mine). I've always found solace in this verse. Trials won't last forever.

During my really rough years, my friends and I agreed to stop saying, "It can't get any worse," because it seemed like it did keep getting worse. We changed the phrase to, "It's going to get better," and *eventually* it did. I endured some tough years before I was able to harvest the joy Peter promised.

In truth, our whole lives are just "a little while."

> *"Our life is like the morning fog—it's here a little while, then it's gone" (James 4:14).*

75

I'm thankful we have a God who understands and tells us He can relate to our trials. He understands that when we are in the middle of a storm, a day can feel like a year. Walk faithfully through the darker days; God has a good harvest planned.

Joy and happiness come in many forms...

The insane humor of a best friend (mine can literally make me laugh over things I should be crying about)

The ability to see past our pain and reach out to help someone else

The way the sun warms us on a spring day

The laughter of a child

Seek out the harvest of joy. Don't put parameters on it. If we tell ourselves, "I'll find joy once such and such happens," we could be missing joy now by locking ourselves into finding it only one way. Life is too multi-dimensional to put in a box. Look eagerly for joy.

PRAYER HARVEST

God loves to answer our prayers. Sure, sometimes the answer is *no* or *wait*, but He still answers them. The closer I've gotten to God, the more I hand over everything to Him. I learned one of my favorite prayers from a wonderful pastor. It begins with "Dear LORD of All Lost Things..." Go ahead and laugh now, but pretty soon, your car keys or credit card will go missing and you'll be on your knees spouting it off. The funniest part is, it actually works! I have to use this one a lot because of my ADOS personality—Attention Deficit...Oooh Shiny. I can get distracted from my distractions.

As a young wife, I led a women's Bible study. The women became my good friends, and we were able to learn and encourage each other in our faith. After a few years, we all started families. Our lives were changing, and we didn't want to stop our weekly meetings, but most of us were strapped for sleep, let alone time to complete a Bible study.

I asked God for a solution, and one day He gave it to me. I thought we could all meet during the day for a prayer group. We could bring our children and pray over them while we were together. Since all of us were stay-at-home moms, we decided on one day a week, alternating homes, where we would meet, pray, and have lunch together.

Each woman would take a turn telling us about her week and her prayer requests. Then we would all pray for her and move on to the next, while stopping in between to change diapers or deal with toddler tantrums as needed. I looked forward to our time together every week.

If we are not careful, distractions or false priorities come between us and our relationship with our heavenly Father.

I'll never forget one of our meetings. My friend admitted she almost didn't come because she woke up in the middle of the night and couldn't go back to sleep for an hour or two. I remember telling her she must have been waking up right when I was finally going to sleep. As the rest of the group started to compare stories, we all realized God had woken each of us up the night before, all of the times overlapping, and as it turned out one of us was awake and praying all night long.

I was in awe of what a wonderful God we serve. We all felt His hand of blessing over our commitment to Him to meet and pray, despite distractions. We saw so many answers to our requests; we were reaping a harvest during our season of prayer.

If we are not careful, distractions or false priorities come between us and our relationship with our heavenly Father. God wants time with us. We need to sit at His feet and soak Him in. Sometimes we need to readjust our mindset about *how* we are supposed to spend time with God, but the important thing is to make it a priority.

Any one of the ladies in our prayer group could have opted out because it was inconvenient at times, but no one did because we each had a solid commitment to God. Looking back, I am proud of the choices we made. God answered so many of our prayers, it makes me wonder what would have happened if we hadn't been praying. God wants to bless us, but we need to do our part and come to Him with our needs and heart's desires.

Get started today. Don't miss out on the prayer harvest!

Make It Personal

1. What gifts do you have that you can contribute to the body of Christ?

2. Can you invite some other women over to start praying or studying God's Word together?

3. Have you considered keeping a Prayer Journal to document God's faithfulness in your life?

11

A Time to Hate (or Severely Dislike)

Hate is one of those words I try to avoid. It always seems so harsh. When my kids use it in reference to something, my immediate response has always been, "We don't hate, we severely dislike." I wouldn't call my solution perfect, but at least it's not that mean "hate" word, right?

You can perhaps imagine then how shocked I was to discover that the word "hate" appears over 150 times in the Bible. Below are just a few examples:

> All who fear the LORD will **hate** evil. Therefore, I **hate** pride and arrogance, corruption and perverse speech (Proverbs 8:13).

> **Hate** evil and love what is good; turn your courts into true halls of justice. Perhaps even yet the LORD God of heaven's Armies will have mercy on the remnant of his people (Amos 5:15).

*Don't just pretend to love others. Really love them. **Hate** what is wrong. Hold tightly to what is good (Romans 12:9). You love justice and **hate** evil. Therefore, O God, your God has anointed you, pouring out the oil of joy on you more than on anyone else (Hebrews 1:9).*

According to God's Word, hating is not evil. God calls us to hate, at least when it comes to evil, but the Bible clearly doesn't give us permission to hate a person. Certain examples of evil in our world quickly come to my mind, such as sexual abuse, torture and mass genocide. Pure evil. The difference between believers and non-believers is, as Christians, we are commanded to love our enemies, but hate the evil they perpetrate.

The question I wrestle with is what to do with this hate? How do I express it in a way that honors God? When I think of these forms of evil, I feel a righteous anger begin to surface. But, is anger ever right or justified? For the answer, we only need to turn to the Word.

The Bibles gives many examples of God becoming angry, especially with His chosen children, the people of Israel, which to me is proof they are His children. I know I'm angrier when my own children disobey than when other children do! A few times, Moses or Abraham interceded when God was angry. Why do you think He shows us His anger? God certainly didn't need Moses or Abraham to dissuade Him from making a bad decision. God is incapable of wrong.

God's anger is just and purposeful. Always has been. Always will be. His anger serves a purpose, whether it is to remind us who is really in charge or provide an opportunity to demonstrate His mercy.

HATE SIN

All four gospels give an account of Jesus clearing the temple following His triumphant entry into Jerusalem for the Passover. These verses are often used to illustrate a show of anger from Jesus. We all get angry. It's an emotion God created for a purpose.

Jesus goes to the temple as soon as He arrives in town, because, even from the young age of twelve when He stayed behind after the departure of the caravan that included His family, He viewed the temple as His home. When Jesus went missing as a young boy, Mary and Joseph found Him in the temple after a frantic search.

> *"...why did you need to search? he asked. 'Didn't you know that I must be in my Father's house?" (Luke 2:49).*

I can relate because my heart is so closely knit to the church in which I grew up. Attending almost every time the doors were open meant I knew every nook and cranny. I made happy memories in almost every room of living life alongside other believers and loving them like brothers and sisters. We weren't perfect, but we were family. The buildings are sacred to me, not because of their brick and mortar, but because they were used to accomplish God's purposes in my life; they felt like home to me. A church or temple is meant to bring glory to God and draw His people together.

Jesus arrives in Jerusalem for Passover amid praise and adoration, yet all the while knowing He is marching towards His painful death. I find the account in the gospel of Mark the most insightful because it mentions Jesus going to the temple as soon as He arrived in Jerusalem (Mark 11:11).

When Jesus entered late in the afternoon, He must have seen the last remnants of a long day of merchant activity. I'm sure some merchant booths had already shut down for the evening and others were in the process of doing the same. Business had come to a close, but the evidence of animals having been sold for sacrifice was ample, with the dung still lying on the floor and the odor permeating the air.

Jesus must have been angry after seeing the temple converted to a marketplace, yet He refrained from doing or saying anything at the time. So often, we are not able to do the same. My anger sparks quick and hot, and, too frequently, I sin in my anger. Thank goodness, Jesus did not follow the "April" model. He sets the standard.

First of all, His anger is justified. God's will is that His temple be used to draw people closer to Him. The temple He entered that day was not just another building. It was the building that housed God Himself before Jesus' resurrection allowed us all direct access to God. Letting it become a place where animals were bought and sold was a desecration of a holy place.

Jesus' anger was also righteous, meaning it was morally right. We should experience a similar anger at the continued demise of a moral standard within our own communities and culture. We should be angry at what makes God angry, such as the murder of innocent babies through abortion, the persecution of believers or the abuse of children to name a few examples. However, we must be careful not to sin in our anger.

We can hate sin, but Jesus shows us we should never hate people.

I imagine Jesus left that night, upset, venting to His disciples about what He had seen. The next morning, Jesus arose knowing it was the day to confront evil. He arrived at the temple and immediately started knocking over tables and chairs and driving out the buyers and sellers.

> *"The Scriptures declare, 'My Temple will be called a house of prayer for all nations,' but you have turned it into a den of thieves" (Mark 11:17).*

Jesus' anger is just and purposeful. He had the absolute authority and right to judge what was happening in His Father's house.

Jesus' anger is also controlled. We know this, because this is the only example we find throughout the Scriptures of Him expressing anger. We are called as Christians to stand up for what is right and not let sin continue unopposed. We can hate sin, but Jesus shows us we should never hate people. He forgave the men who murdered Him while He was dying on the cross for their very souls.

HATE OUR ENEMY?

Jesus understood enemies. Everywhere He went, He ran into people who would do anything to stop His ministry, anything to stop Him.

It is sad when a person we were once close to and loved becomes our worst enemy. The pendulum of emotion swings just as high on both sides of love and pain. The amount of love we feel for someone seems to be proportionate to the amount of pain they can cause us. The deeper the love, the deeper the pain we feel.

It's easy to get caught up in our pain and let the hurt come out in anger and hate. Unfortunately, if we allow hate to permeate us, it changes us, and not in a good way. Hate begins when we see only the negatives and forget all the positives. We no longer look at the person or situation objectively and tend to want to rewrite our history, taking out the pieces that don't fit into our new perspective.

A strange new phenomenon is taking place around our country—divorce parties. In the same way friends and family come together to celebrate a wedding, they join to celebrate a divorce. Believe me, I understand when divorce is the best option for your circumstances, but I can't say it is something to celebrate. Divorce causes irreparable harm, even when it is necessary. It doesn't bring joy to God's heart, and I don't think it should bring joy to ours either. If we are so filled with hate for someone that we celebrate the death of that relationship, it's time to reevaluate our own heart.

We don't have to be divorced to hate a spouse either. Hatred might be even more common in unhealthy, unhappy marriages than it is in divorce. No marriage is perfect, and no spouse is either. However, guarding our heart against hate is vital in our relationship with our spouse and our relationship with God. Someone once told me that the people in life who are the hardest to love are usually the people who need to be loved the most. I've found that statement to be very true. So, are we the hardest one to love or are we the one who is called to go above and beyond in loving the unlovely? We are at least one, if not both.

> But God showed his great love for us by sending Christ to die
> for us while we were still sinners (Romans 5:8).

God chose to love us instead of hate us when He had plenty of reason to hate. Since we are called to be Christ-like, we must also lay down our reasons to hate and choose love. This doesn't mean we allow people to treat us in abusive ways. Instead, it means we choose to pray for our enemies and not let hate commandeer our hearts. We can hate what a person does, but that doesn't mean we hate the person. We must remember who the real enemy is…Satan.

HATE INJUSTICE

> **Hate** evil and love what is good; turn your courts into true
> halls of justice (Amos 5:15).

Based on this verse, it appears courts have always battled dispensing true justice. God is the only righteous Judge, and every other one is found lacking. I hate the inequity that sometimes exists in our court system. "Hate" is a strong term, but it fits. Unfortunately, after plenty of experience working within the system, I find evil can run rampant there. I have had good and bad days in court, but my frustration mainly comes from the lack of common sense in the process. Thankfully, we have a God who is above every judge and can turn any judge or "king's heart like water" (Proverbs 21:1). He can easily change the flow of thoughts and decisions.

Before participating in the judicial process in our country, I naively believed truth would always prevail and the courts were focused on finding the truth. I now know justice is not something we can count on while here on earth. Justice will come one day through THE righteous and perfect judge. This is not to say earthly judges never rule with wisdom and discernment; they may or they may not. We can guarantee, however, that God will judge perfectly.

Our system is flawed, too often devoid of true godly wisdom and, in the quest to protect, can offer more rights to the perpetrators of crimes than to the victims. Children especially are at a disadvantage. Their word matters little when compared to an adult's. My desire is for truth to win out, regardless of age. The silver lining is that the failures of our courts force us to lean hard into God and trust in HIM, not any man-made system.

My life is living proof that God can and does prevail, even in a flawed system. With God's help, I walked away from using lawyers and fought one of the biggest battles possible in the courts, requesting the removal of all of my former husband's parenting time. And I won—not because of anything I did, but because of how God orchestrated every detail. The only superpowers I have access to are the power of prayer and trust in God, regardless of the outcome.

Our God is a God who saves. He is worthy! Praise His name!

Make It Personal

1. What do you hate? Do you think God hates it as well?

2. How can you express hate in a godly way?

3. Has hate clouded your view of the past? Ask God to clear the clouds.

12

A Time to Heal

Life can change in an instant. When my daughter Ainsley was about eleven, we were spending the evening socializing at a friend's house. All of the adults were chatting in the back of the house, while the kids were dancing it up in the front room. Apparently, their dancing included jumping off the coffee table.

The house was full of music, laughter and fun until those sounds were punctuated by screams. I ran to the front room and found Ainsley on the floor, unable to move from her waist down. She had slipped off the table and hit her back in the fall.

As I rushed to her side, my friend ran to the phone and dialed 9-1-1. My child's eyes were full of shock and fear. I told myself this couldn't be real, she would be moving in just a second, but the seconds became minutes and her fear increased. I spent those minutes while we waited for the ambulance trying to calm her down and reassure her.

When the emergency team rushed in, they surrounded her and began running tests, asking if she could feel anything. I could see them running a sharp object from her heel to the top of her foot with absolutely no response or reflex of any kind. They brought in a stabilization board and strapped her down. She started panicking. I dropped to my knees and put my hand on her head and began praying out loud. I knew this was completely out of my hands, and we desperately needed Jesus. *Please, Jesus, heal my sweet girl and bring peace to her heart.*

In the next few minutes, they had to start an IV before transporting her, causing her anxiety level to increase even more. When they pricked her, her legs moved slightly, giving us the first sign of hope. However, she still had no feeling or control.

We rode in the ambulance to the children's hospital, and they wheeled her into the emergency room on the gurney. I stayed as close to her as they would allow, which was in the corner of the room. I felt like I was watching an episode of ER as they swarmed around her, running tests and asking her questions. As one doctor talked with her to distract her, one was running another sharp object up her foot, and another was roughly twisting the flesh on her legs. Again, there was no response. I had the distinct feeling that life as we had always known it might be changed forever. I did the only thing I knew to do to help my daughter—I fervently prayed.

Over the next few minutes, Ainsley slowly began responding to some of the tests. Praise God, within only an hour or so, the feeling returned to her legs. We *both* were literally *walking* out of the hospital a few hours later. Our God is an awesome Healer. Miracles happen every day. We just need eyes to see them.

CRIPPLING PAIN

One Sabbath day as Jesus was teaching in a synagogue, he saw a woman who had been crippled by an evil spirit. She had been bent double for eighteen years and was unable to stand up straight. When Jesus saw her, he called her over and said, "Dear woman, you are healed of your sickness!" Then he

touched her, and instantly she could stand straight. How she
praised God! (Luke 13:10-13).

This woman's time for healing had *finally* come, after eighteen years. Can you imagine waiting eighteen years for healing? That is the amount of time it takes from giving birth to a child all the way until you get to kick them out of your house…I mean, until they leave for college.

Notice how this woman was called over by Jesus. She may have given up on being healed, but God had a plan. He saw her pain, the same way He sees ours. Her eighteen years of discomfort served a purpose as her story will forever give God the glory through His word.

Miracles happen everyday. We just need eyes to see them.

Eighteen years is a long time to wait for physical healing and, thankfully, most of us have probably never been in the position of needing healing for that long. However, when we throw emotional healing, relationship healing and spiritual healing into the mix, I'm guessing eighteen years becomes a number many of us can relate to.

In actuality, many of us were hurt as children or young adults and still haven't received healing because we haven't dealt with the pain. We ignore it, run from it, deny it—basically, we do just about anything to avoid facing it. The problem with those solutions is that true healing hasn't taken place. Would you rather just "cope" with your past or receive healing?

I'm going to be honest; at times my own answer to that question has been "cope," mostly because I wasn't seeing the true cost. When I started factoring in that my coping was only forcing my family and friends to pay the price, all of a sudden I didn't feel so prideful about my awesome coping skills.

Are we really coping or are we simply delaying healing? Maybe you can relate to one or more of the following:

- *My spouse cheated on me, so I'm justified in never trusting anyone again.*

- *My parent abandoned me, so prove to me over and over and over again that you are never going to leave me.*
- *I need to have control in every situation; it's the only way for me to feel safe.*
- *I'm not going to love you the way you need to be loved, because I'm too busy protecting myself from ever being hurt by you.*
- *I need you to fill my love tank all the time, even though I admit it has a leak in it someone else created. I'm too busy to fix it, so you need to keep pouring and pouring and pouring into me.*
- *I don't want to be honest with you because that might mean we will have a conflict, so I'll just pretend things don't bother me, when they really do, and then I'll blow up at you.*
- *God will fix me. I don't have to actively engage myself in my healing.*

Don't misunderstand the last one. I absolutely believe God can and does perform miraculous healings; obviously He did for my daughter. I also believe some Christians don't realize they need healing, while others use their Christianity as an excuse to avoid facing pain in their past. They refuse to participate in their own healing and hide behind pride that they don't need "fixing."

It wasn't until Nathan came to David and confronted him about committing adultery with Bathsheba (2 Samuel 12) that David repented and received emotional and spiritual healing. Often we are unable to see our sin or the baggage we carry from our painful past. Admittedly, while many of us don't initially act like David and accept the truth others speak over us, we need someone else to reveal what they see in us.

Once we own our behavior or actions, it results in the opportunity to learn, grow and experience healing. If we keep pretending we don't have any problems or issues, we only hurt our loved ones and ourselves as well as forfeit the opportunity for healing.

When you look throughout Scripture at miraculous healings, there were times when people literally touched Jesus' cloak and were healed; but there were also times when Jesus required something of the person in need of healing. Let's look at some of Jesus' healings together.

HEALING BARTIMAEUS OF BLINDNESS

As Jesus and a large crowd were leaving Jericho, Bartimaeus, a blind beggar, was sitting by the roadside. When he heard that it was Jesus of Nazareth passing by, he shouted to Jesus to have mercy on him. Although many told him to keep quiet, he shouted louder. Jesus stood still and called Bartimaeus to Him. Throwing off his cloak, the man sprang up and came to Jesus, asking Jesus to let him see again. Jesus said to him, "Go; your faith has made you well." Immediately Bartimaeus regained his sight and followed Jesus on His way. (See Mark 10:46-52.)

Bartimaeus shouted, screamed and ran to Jesus begging for healing. We need to ask ourselves, if Jesus were walking past us today, what would we beg Him to heal in our lives? I'd have a hard time picking only one thing. The only requirement for this miracle was asking for it and the faith to believe Jesus could do it. Do we have enough faith to ask?

HEALING A MAN BORN BLIND

Jesus saw a man who was blind from birth. He then spat on the ground and made mud with the saliva and spread the mud on the man's eyes, telling him to go wash in the pool of Siloam. The man did this, and his sight was restored. (See John 9:1-41)

This man knew he needed healing, and when God used an

91

unconventional method to heal him, he embraced it. Are we willing to embrace an unconventional method to receive our healing?

HEALING A PARALYTIC

A large crowd had assembled around the house where Jesus was staying in Capernaum. With no room left in or outside the house, four men dug through the roof and lowered a paralyzed man on a mat down through the roof right in front of Jesus. When Jesus saw how strongly they believed that He would help, Jesus said to the sick man, "Son, your sins are forgiven!" Some of the Jewish leaders thought this was blasphemy, for only God can forgive sins. Jesus let them know that the Son of Man has authority on earth to forgive sins, and He said to the paralytic, "I say to you, stand up, take your mat and go home." The man stood up, took the mat and went out before all of them, so that they were all amazed and glorified God, saying, "We have never seen anything like this." (See Matthew 9:1-8; Mark 2:1-12; Luke 5:18-26.)

Never forget the spiritual battle being waged constantly.

Fight back!

Have we asked our close friends to pray for our healing? If the paralytic in this story had told his friends not to go to all the trouble necessary to get him in front of Jesus, not only would he have missed his healing, but everyone would have missed out on the opportunity to see God glorified. We need to let our friends help carry us to the cross.

Jesus is obviously capable of healing us physically, emotionally, spiritually and mentally. It's not a "one size fits all" solution though. Our God loves us individually and knows the plan He has for each one of us—plans to prosper us and give us a hope and a future (Jeremiah 29:11).

SATAN LOVES TO INTERFERE

Sometimes we have a difficult time interpreting physical pain through the spiritual realm. A woman in my prayer group struggled with neck pain and was repeatedly seeing a chiropractor. She came one day asking us to pray for her healing; her trips to the chiropractor were putting a strain on her family. When we began seeing how Satan was using this neck pain to bring discord into her life, it was like a light bulb went off. Satan was the author of the pain. We immediately went to the Lord in prayer, asking for Satan to be bound and that he would no longer be able to use her body in this way. The pain immediately left her and didn't return.

So often, we immediately rush to the doctor or our medicine cabinet for the cure and fail to recognize Satan at work. Believe me, I am as guilty of this as anyone. With three children, when I see any sign of sickness, I rush to medicate, hoping to ward off whatever possible illness is heading our way. But Satan is in the business of using whatever he can in order to draw us away from God or bring conflict to distract and discourage us. Satan makes it *personal* too. He will *personally* attack you. If you don't believe me, read the first two chapters of Job. Never forget the spiritual battle being waged constantly. Fight back. One way is to follow the instructions James gives us for healing.

> *Are any of you sick? You should call for the elders of the church to come and pray over you, anointing you with oil in the name of the Lord. Such a prayer offered in faith will heal the sick, and the Lord will make you well. And if you have committed any sins, you will be forgiven. Confess your sins to each other and pray for each other so that you may be healed. The earnest prayer of a righteous person has great power and produces wonderful results (James 5:14-16).*

It seems many Christians gloss over these verses. Why don't we ask to be anointed with oil and receive prayer? Is it a lack of faith? Is it the fear our faith can't withstand Jesus' answer being "no" or "not yet"?

We want to believe. We want to have faith in Jesus' ability to heal and yet, there is often an inner struggle because of the chance, even after acting in faith and believing in healing, His answer may still not be what we want. When faced with God's "no" or "not yet," I choose to believe in God's omniscience and trust He has a better ending to the story, even when I can't understand it. Get some anointing oil, pray in faith, and believe God's outcome is the best one.

We all need some form of healing in our lives. Let's never forget Jesus is the Healer.

Make It Personal

1. In what areas do you need healing? (physical, emotional, spiritual, mental)

2. Have you run to Jesus and begged Him for healing?

3. What unconditional methods for healing are available?

4. Have you reached out to friends and asked for their help/prayers for healing?

13

A Time to Keep

To Keep.

Keep on.

Keep it up.

Keep pace.

Keep time.

For keeps.

Keep house.

The dictionary lists twenty-six definitions for the word *keep,* not including all of the idioms or phrases connected to the word. With all of these different ways of using one word, it won't be surprising that "keep" is used 450 times in the Bible.[1]

Keep the way of the Lord (Genesis 18:19).

Keep the Sabbath holy (Exodus 20:8).

Keep all of my decrees (Leviticus 20:8).

---

[1] In the NKJV

Keep your word (Numbers 32:20).

He keeps every promise forever (Psalm 146:6).

Keep in perfect peace (Isaiah 26:3).

Keep on asking.

Keep on seeking.

Keep on knocking (Matthew 7:7).

For me, to "keep" calls me to consistency, mainly in areas that are challenging for me. I don't have to remind myself to "keep" loving my children or "keep" eating cheesecake. I do those things without anyone making me or reminding me because I love them. Yes, both my children and cheesecake.

The command "to keep" implies a non-natural inclination for me. It calls me to action in areas I might otherwise neglect. God commands us *"to keep the way of the Lord"* (Genesis 18:19). In all honesty, my nature is to be selfish and to avoid pain. However, I find God calls me over and over again to painful places that require me to take the focus off of myself and place it on Him.

Sometimes God asks us to persist during difficult circumstances. In the last months of my first marriage, I was leading a Beth Moore Bible study where she brought up the story in Acts 14, where Paul is beat unconscious, dragged out of the city gates and left for dead. Scripture says believers then gathered around Paul, and he got up and went back into the town. One of the questions in the Bible study was whether or not we would have gone back into the city if we had been in Paul's shoes.

At our next Bible study, I detected a slight reluctance from the group to share their answers, assuming it was because it was one of our first meetings. I decided, as the leader, I would go first to get things started. My answer had been, "Yes, I would get up and go back into the city." After I shared, we went around the room and every other woman in our group answered. One by one, they all said, "No, I wouldn't have gone back."

Later that night, I started mulling over my answer. Was my response only what I thought God wanted to hear or was "yes" my real answer? After my contemplation, I reaffirmed to God that "yes" was my real answer because when He tells me to do something, no matter how hard, my desire is to obey Him. I have tasted and experienced the blessings of obedience and wouldn't want to sacrifice those blessings out of fear.

The story doesn't end there though. A few weeks later, I had one of the worst evenings ever with my then husband. After getting into my car and driving around the corner, I parked and literally starting screaming at God in between my sobs. More than anything, I did not want to go back home. What I wanted was to run as far away as possible. I remember crying out over and over, "Don't make me go back, don't make me go back…"

After calming down, I reached into my backseat to search for my Bible, and instead my hand found my Bible study book. Hoping to find some comfort, I opened it and saw my earlier answer to the question of whether I would go back into the city after being abused. I felt God asking me, "Did you really mean it when you answered yes?" I could feel a heaviness in the air. It was just God and I. It was my "Paul" moment.

I breathed out a quiet, "Yes, I did" knowing God was asking me to go back home. It took every ounce of determination and faith to walk back in and keep on going. God may be asking you to keep going in the face of some horrible circumstances. Let me encourage you to keep on being obedient to God. The safest place for us is in the center of God's will, regardless of the storm raging around us.

PERSISTENCE MAKES THE DIFFERENCE

Many times I find myself trying to keep to a schedule, keep to a commitment, or keep to a healthy diet and the biggest difficulty with accomplishing my goal is ME. Can I get an "Amen?" Anyone can make a commitment, but those who actually keep a challenging commitment are few and far between. Persistence makes the difference. When I need to see an encouraging dose of persistence, I go to Luke 18.

> *One day Jesus told his disciples a story to show that they should always pray and never give up. "There was a judge in a certain city," he said, "who neither feared God nor cared about people. A widow of that city came to him repeatedly, saying, "Give me justice in this dispute with my enemy." The judge ignored her for a while, but finally he said to himself, "I don't fear God or care about people, but this woman is driving me crazy. I'm going to see that she gets justice, because she is wearing me out with her constant requests!"*

> *Then the Lord said, "Learn a lesson from this unjust judge. Even he rendered a just decision in the end. So don't you think God will surely give justice to his chosen people who cry out to him day and night? Will he keep putting them off? I tell you, he will grant justice to them quickly!" (Luke 18: 1-8).*

This woman came repeatedly to the judge. If she had given up sooner, she never would have received justice. God asks us to "cry out to Him day and night." I have had the experience of having to rely on an unjust judge for a ruling that would severely impact my family. This saint's example shows how important it is to keep persevering. Don't give up.

KEEP ASKING, KEEP SEEKING, KEEP BELIEVING

My special needs daughter, Jerilyn, has always presented as a complex case diagnostically for her doctors. She was six before we made it to the front of the line for testing with a developmental pediatrician, specializing in autism. He was connected to a teaching hospital and very often would invite students or other professionals into our appointments. He readily admitted Jerilyn was one of his most difficult patients to diagnose and treat, even with his twenty-five years of experience.

Her diagnosis continually changes. Every doctor or psychiatrist gives us a different opinion. This has made finding the best educational environment challenging. She started kindergarten in a regular education classroom where she had only two conversations with peers the entire year. We repeated kindergarten with some improvement, but still saw the widening gap between her and the other children.

Persistence makes the difference.

Parents of special needs students understand the overwhelming world of IEP's (Individual Education Plans). An IEP is a legal document the school is required to follow for your child's unique educational needs.

The school district we were in did not make it easy to have her needs met. She went into first grade still hiding under tables and requiring much of the teacher's attention. I had to keep pushing for a different solution. After two and a half years, the district agreed to place her in a self-contained class in the Emotionally/Behaviorally Delayed (EBD) program. Although I wasn't convinced this was where she needed to be, it meant increased attention and an individualized plan specifically for her, which she desperately needed.

After almost three years in EBD, it was necessary to make another change. We moved to Arizona and discovered they had a high-functioning autism program, which we hoped would better meet Jerilyn's needs. It did, for a while, but then we found ourselves searching again for a better solution.

DON'T GIVE UP!

When Jerilyn was in sixth grade and still operating on a second grade level, I decided it was time to become an IEP expert and have my child placed in a school specifically designed to meet her educational needs. There is a learning curve as the parent of a child with a disability. You cannot be knowledgeable about everything at once, but eventually you will be a life-trained psychiatrist, dietician, behavior coach, tutor, triage nurse, therapist, IEP expert and the list keeps growing.

As any parent with a special needs student understands, these IEP meetings don't always go in our direction. It can feel like a tug of war. The school is advocating for as many of the district dollars to stay within their purse. The parent is advocating for their child's best interests. This is not to imply the schools don't want a successful solution for a child; it's just that they have to weigh the costs, and agreeing on the "best solution" can be difficult at times. Many parents are forced to hire an advocate or legal representative to ensure their child receives the services they desperately need.

I planned on having a whole team at our next IEP meeting to advocate for Jerilyn; her behavioral therapist, disability specialists, education specialists and her intensive case manager. However, they all started cancelling on me at the last minute, and when I walked into the meeting, only one of my "team" was able to attend.

I was so discouraged and began second-guessing my decision to forego hiring a formal advocate to come with me, literally holding back the tears during the first ten minutes of the meeting. I felt defeated, and we had only just begun.

Usually a fighter when it comes to my kids' needs, I had no fight left in me that morning, when I desperately needed it. As the school went over their results from all their testing, they kept using terms that made me feel like they were going to attempt to leave her in the current program while incorporating some new supports.

Then the discussion changed from test results to placement options. Her school psychologist opened up the opportunity for me to explain why I felt the particular school I wanted was the best fit for Jerilyn. Although the district representative had a few more questions and an additional placement suggestion, she eventually agreed the school I chose was the best option for Jerilyn. The new school would have cost me $25,000 a year, and now the district would be funding it.

I call this my "Gideon moment" because God didn't need a "team" of people to fight the battle. He sent me into that meeting at my weakest moment so even I couldn't steal any of His glory—in the same way Gideon went into battle with only 300 men against an army too numerous to count and came out victorious (Judges 6-8). When we keep asking, seeking and believing, God is able to show us great and mighty victories.

KEEP IT UP

Whatever mountain is in front of you, keep climbing. Keep a steady focus on God. Keep on trusting Him for the solution. Keep on believing His plan is best. Keep reading His Word. Keep praying. Keep on doing housework—oh, wait, I could surely live without that one. Well...I suppose I couldn't live without it. I just don't want it to be done by me. The one real solution I can come up with...house-cleaning fairies, obviously! Until they arrive, I'm going to keep on asking for them. Keep on seeking them out. And keep on waiting for their knock on my door.

Make It Personal

1. What experiences in your life have forced you to "keep" persevering? What was the end result of your perseverance?

2. Have you ever experienced a "Gideon" moment? What was it?

3. Complete the following phrase—I need to keep (fill in the blank). Now, go do it!

14

A Time to Kill

Have you ever wondered why they kill a horse after it breaks a leg? I have. "A Time to Kill" led me to research the reasoning behind the practice. It takes twelve to sixteen weeks for a horse's broken leg to heal, and no weight can be placed on the leg while it is in the healing process. This is an impossible requirement for a horse that must stand on all four legs. If a surgery is attempted, it often results in the horse reinjuring the leg immediately as it makes an attempt to stand up. In this scenario, the most merciful option is death.

I'm an Old Testament gal—not in the sense that I don't adore the new covenant explained in the New Testament, just based on the fact that I absolutely love the Old Testament. What I love most about it is getting to know the people more intimately. The Old Testament gives you the frame of reference for a whole life lived loving God, with all the ups and downs that go with it. You see it in the lives of Abraham, Moses, David, Job and Solomon among others. We also see great examples of women of faith in the Old Testament such as Ruth, Esther, Hannah and Bathsheba.

One of the more difficult things to understand in the Old Testament is

God's commands to go and kill every man, woman and child in a nation. Destroy it. Leave nothing and no one. It is challenging to understand that the same God of limitless mercy and abounding love who sent His son to die for me also calls for the killing of entire populations.

One year, while I was reading through the Old Testament, I started to cry out to God about this call to kill. I wanted to understand. Slowly, things started occurring to me as I would read. First, the Bible tells us there is nothing new under the sun. People have always struggled with evil. Think of Joseph Stalin, Adolf Hitler and Sadaam Hussein. No generation escapes evil. Satan is a roaring lion seeking whom he can devour…and he has been in the business of evil ever since the world began.

On some level, I can understand why evil people must be killed or destroyed to save others. This is why capitol punishment exists. "An eye for an eye." Logically, if we believe by killing one person we will be saving the lives of many others, it feels justifiable. But…how could God require the *innocents* to also be killed?

I think this is an important question to be able to answer, especially when asked by unbelievers. In order to answer it, let's take a walk through the biblical account of King Agag. Agag was the king of the Amalekites, and God told the Israelite's King Saul to annihilate every Amalekite man, woman, child and even animal.

> *And the Lord sent you on a mission and told you, "Go and*
> *completely destroy the sinners, the Amalekites, until they are*
> *all dead" (1 Samuel 15:18).*

God referred to the Amalekites as an evil people. Historically, they were known to sacrifice their own babies to their god, Molech, by placing the infants in his fiery clutches. Against God's command, King Saul decided to spare King Agag along with all the animals.

The prophet, Samuel, confronted King Saul, who gave the excuse that they were planning to sacrifice the animals to God. Samuel assured Saul that

God wanted obedience, not sacrifice. Right there and then, Samuel killed King Agag. However, later on in Scripture, we discover Saul must have spared other Amalekites as well because their nation began to grow again.

Unfortunately, Saul's failure to destroy every Amalekite led to new generations raised with hatred towards God's people and a desire to avenge their past. Over 500 years later, Haman the Agagite, a presumed descendent of King Agag, was behind the decree to kill all the Jews during the time of Esther. Interestingly, Mordecai, the man Haman focused his hate upon, was a descendant of King Saul. The two people groups faced each other yet again. If King Saul had followed through on God's initial command, future lives would have been saved. God sees a much bigger picture than we are ever able to see.

It is in God's mercy that He commands anything. He desires for all to come to Him.

My personal opinion is that there is an age of accountability for everyone regarding salvation. I don't claim to know what it is, because I believe it is different for everyone, but that age is when a person comes face to face with the truth of the Gospel of Christ and makes a decision to believe or not believe. The choices don't include "maybe later," or "I'll have to think about it," because those options are actually a choice not to believe. Not a single person is guaranteed a tomorrow here on Earth. However, if we die before our age of accountability, my belief is that we are ushered into heaven.

If we look at things from an eternal perspective, it is in God's mercy that He commands anything. He desires for all to come to Him, but let's face it— He knows who will and who won't. Which is more merciful? A finite end to an evil nation such as the Amalekites, where everyone had either reached their age of accountability and chosen to reject the one true God, or had never reached that age and would therefore be welcomed into heaven; or allow *many* more to be born into a nation choosing a destructive path away from God and subsequently away from an eternity in heaven?

PERSECUTION IS ALIVE AND WELL

Although God is always merciful, Satan is intent on stealing, killing and destroying—without mercy. My life has been threatened multiple times, and in a strange way I'm not even surprised by it anymore. God revealed to me that the devil is really the one intent on killing me, and he is eager to use anyone willing to lob threats at me. This taught me a few things:

- Satan wants me dead because I pose a threat to his kingdom of darkness by sharing God's light.
- God is *way* more powerful, and I need not fear that Satan can supersede God's plan for my life.
- It freed me to realize who the real enemy is and forgive those who are unknowingly being used by Satan to attack me.

When we are walking in our God-given purpose, God's Word assures us we will be persecuted, but it doesn't follow with permission to respond in vengeance. In fact, the Bible commands quite the opposite.

> *God blesses you when people mock you and persecute you and lie about you and say all sorts of evil things against you because you are my followers. Be happy about it! Be very glad! For a great reward awaits you in heaven. And remember, the ancient prophets were persecuted in the same way...But I say, love your enemies! Pray for those who persecute you (Matthew 5:11-12, 44).*

We must guard our minds and not let hate or depression take root. Someone may be making life unbearable right now. However, if we find ourselves contemplating how to hurt ourselves or someone else, reach out; it is time to seek help immediately. (See Appendix A.) God adores you...don't ever forget that. People want to help you—don't let Satan tell you lies to the contrary.

God has ordained each one of our days (Psalms 139:16), and every day that He wakes us up and gives us breath in our lungs is a day He has given us to live. God always has perfect timing, and He has a plan for the end. God's Word lets us know there will be a final ending to this world once Jesus returns. In Revelation 6:2, Jesus rides in on a white horse, ready for battle.

At any moment, the clouds could part. I look around some days at the destruction existing all around us, whether it be a child that is kidnapped, a woman raped, or genocide occurring in another country and wonder why God is waiting. The only answer my heart can understand is that He is waiting for one last soul to submit. It's because of His mercy.

We serve a merciful God. In His mercy, He saved me. In His mercy, He wants to save you. In His mercy, He wants to save everyone.

CIRCLE OF LIFE

One Christmas, my daughter Jerilyn found a five-and-a-half-foot gopher snake in the desert area behind our house. She caught it and walked around with it hanging from her neck for days. I know many of you are probably feeling squeamish and thinking, *Please, please, please tell me that you made her get rid of it*…but not so much.

Over the years, Jerilyn has brought every kind of animal to my doorstep, and I've ceased being afraid of them. I've even come to the conclusion that snakes make good pets, primarily because they require so little care as opposed to dogs, cats, etc.

I would make her go put the snake back in the desert at night, but it always was close to where she left it the next morning. Really close. One night she decided it was probably cold, so she snuck out and literally slept on the porch sofa with it. (I know…I'm shuddering right along with you.)

Her birthday was right around the corner, and she begged me to allow her to keep it. At first I said no, but the girl is pretty convincing. I conceded and went out to spend the $150 it would take to get a cage and everything else the snake would need, including food. We tried unsuccessfully to get it to eat an already deceased mouse, so we had to go back for the live version. Jerilyn assured me she could do this.

After placing the doomed mouse in the tank with the snake, I covered it so the snake could have some privacy...all right, that's a lie. I covered it because I couldn't watch that go down, literally or figuratively. The next morning, I checked and found the mouse gone. Whew. I went to find Jerilyn and tell her, but couldn't find her. Eventually, I discovered her playing in her closet...with the mouse. "Mom, I named him Squeakers. Isn't he so cute?" She had "rescued" him.

I tried to explain that in order for the snake to live, the mouse must die. It's the circle of life. In the end, she let the snake go free, and the mouse lived in the pricey cage. This life lesson was not an easy one for her...the lover of *all* animals. However, it makes me think of how Christ willingly sacrificed His life, because He is the lover of *all* of us. His blood ran in crimson streams. Don't waste it. Holiness requires sacrifice. We are made complete and whole when we embrace and accept that His death gave us life.

Make It Personal

1. How has God been merciful to you?

2. In what ways can you show mercy to those in your life?

3. What type of persecution do you see in your life? In our country? In the world?

4. Have you ever wanted to hurt yourself or anyone else? If so, don't wait another day. Seek help. (See Appendix A.)

15

A Time to Laugh

I find it ironic that when I organized these chapters in alphabetical order, "A Time to Kill" came right before "A Time to Laugh." Oh, the irony. Let's face it, though, sometimes what is supposed to make us cry ends up making us laugh. A perfect example is when my youngest was about two. One of her many allergies is to peanuts. She was staying at a neighbor's house while I ran an errand. I returned to discover she was having a reaction to a bite of peanut butter-flavored cereal. Red spots were already popping up on her face. By the time I rushed her home, her breathing was sounding labored. After getting through to her specialist's office, they told me to inject her with the EpiPen immediately. Not being the kind of person who assumes the worst, I asked the nurse if she thought it was really necessary. "Yes! Do you know where an EpiPen is?" she screamed through the phone.

Although already scared, now I went into full panic mode. My adrenalin was flowing, ramping up every second. I ran around looking for our EpiPen. Just imagine a chicken with its head cut off. As I'm searching, the nurse is explaining how to use the pen and how my daughter was going cry because it would be painful, but necessary. EpiPen in hand, I removed the protective cover and read the three simple instructions written directly on it. I read them once, twice, three times and could make no sense of them. Too much adrenalin combined with too much fear made me unable to connect my brain to what was obviously English but might as well have been a foreign language. Surely the pharmacy didn't give me the Swahili version, right? All the while, the nurse, who obviously wished she were handling this instead of me, is shouting through the phone, "Just give her the EpiPen!"

Fine! I take off the cap, aim for Daisy's upper thigh and jab the EpiPen in. No….crying. While my brain processes her lack of tears, the pain hits me. I shout into the phone, "Oh. My. Gosh. I just shot it into *my* thumb! Oooowwwww!!" The needle came out the wrong end!! Okay, maybe not the real wrong end, but definitely *not* the one I expected.

Intense pain, coupled with epinephrine AND adrenalin are now coursing through my panicked body. I pull out the needle, which is now bent at a 90-degree angle after hitting a bone in my thumb. I start bleeding and the nurse, not missing a beat, shouts over my cries of pain, "Do you have another EpiPen?" My heart is literally racing a mile a minute as I run to my car to get the extra one I kept there.

Unfortunately, Daisy now understands what is coming. She knows enough to try to squirm away from me, and I know enough to understand the cap on the EpiPen covers the trigger end, not the needle end. Apparently, there was a reason they put those tester pens in the box and maybe, just maybe, I shouldn't have made fun of it when I originally opened it and thought, "*How hard could this possibly be?*" Pride always comes before the fall…or the shot, in this case.

This time, the needle went into my daughter's leg and immediately stopped her allergic reaction. Whew! Safe at last, thank God Almighty, we were safe at last. The nurse reassured me my daughter should be fine, but that we still needed to call 9-1-1 and have them come out to check on her.

It would be great if the story ended there with me saving the day—you know, after I almost ruined the day. But no, that would be someone else's life, not ours. Instead, the next scene in our Lifetime movie includes my ex-husband pulling up to pick up the girls for his weekend visit at the same time the ambulance rolls in.

Oh, joy! The EMTs check my daughter and pronounce her fine. Meanwhile, my thumb is throbbing and I am having a hard time thinking about anything other than the pain, but with my ex standing next to me, there is no way I am going to tell the emergency workers about it. I could see him holding it against me the next time we're in court, and what defense would I have? "Yeah, I was trying to save my daughter's life and instead shot myself in the thumb." I'm not winning any Mother-of-the-Year awards for that one! So I suffered in silence. The EMTs departed, and my daughters left with their father.

Hours later, I headed over to my friend's house and mentioned my thumb, which by this time was totally white and cold. She touched it, pronounced it "dead," and suggested I go to the ER. My response was something like, "Well, that's not happening." Instead, I called Fred, my best friend's husband, who just so happened to be a Physician's Assistant in an ER. He also informed me that I needed to go to an ER because people have lost their thumbs from this. The good news was that I was not alone in my stupidity; the bad news was that I was still way too prideful to consider going to an ER and risk *someone* discovering what I had done. I told Fred to come up with another plan.

Thank goodness God has more grace than I have pride!

Fred called me back with Plan B, which required me to test out my skin by pressing it down and seeing how many seconds it would take to come back up. He said if it took four seconds or more I would need to go to the ER so they could inject me with something to counteract the epinephrine. It took three and a half seconds, so I called it good and hung up. Nope...no need to go in.

Thank goodness God had more grace than I have pride or I would be thumb-less today. Obviously, my ego has taken a back seat since then because I am willing to laugh at myself and share this not-so-stellar moment with all of you.

GOD DEFINITELY HAS A SENSE OF HUMOR

God blessed us with the ability to laugh—at ourselves, at others, at the world around us.

> *A cheerful heart is good medicine, but a crushed spirit dries up the bones (Proverbs 17:22).*

I am very thankful God blessed me with the friends He did, because even on my darkest days they make me laugh. One of my favorite quotes is from the movie *Steel Magnolias*. "Laughter through tears is my favorite emotion." It's so true...at least for women. I'm not sure men would agree. Seems to be a female thing.

I know God has a sense of humor. It's quite obvious given the circumstances that assault my life at times—like the scenario above. That could have happened any day, any time, but the timing is funny. God is all over the timing of our lives. Have you ever had moments when you told someone you would "never" do something...only to find yourself doing it shortly after?

When you say you'll never get pregnant…

When you brag about never getting a ticket…

When you say your child would *never* do that…

When you think a tester EpiPen is superfluous…

God laughs—probably out loud—when we make these proclamations, and all the angels probably look over and wonder what that was all about. It's not that He gets joy from anything that causes us pain, because He doesn't. But when my five-year-old daughter told me that boys are gross and she is never going to like them...I laughed.

In the previous chapter, I mentioned the story of Esther and how Haman was a descendent of the Agagites. God's sense of humor comes out as He deals with this enemy of the Jews.

> The king said, "Who is in the court?" Now Haman had just entered the outer court of the palace to speak to the king about impaling Mordecai on the pole he had set up for him.
>
> His attendants answered, "Haman is standing in the court."
>
> "Bring him in," the king ordered.
>
> When Haman entered, the king asked him, "What should be done for the man the king delights to honor?"
>
> Now Haman thought to himself, "Who is there that the king would rather honor than me?" So he answered the king, "For the man the king delights to honor, have them bring a royal robe the king has worn and a horse the king has ridden, one with a royal crest placed on its head. Then let the robe and horse be entrusted to one of the king's most noble princes. Let them robe the man the king delights to honor, and lead him on the horse through the city streets, proclaiming before him, 'This is what is done for the man the king delights to honor!' "
>
> "Go at once," the king commanded Haman. "Get the robe and the horse and do just as you have suggested for Mordecai the Jew, who sits at the king's gate. Do not neglect anything you have recommended." So Haman got the robe and the horse. He robed Mordecai, and led him on horseback through the city streets, proclaiming before him, "This is what is done for the man the king delights to honor!" (Esther 6:4-11).

I don't know about you, but I got a good chuckle out of this. Can you imagine your enemy having to drive you around, while using a megaphone to tell the world how wonderful you are? Haman's pride was so inflated he assumed the reward would go to him, only to have to be the one who offered all the perks to his enemy. The Bible even says Haman went home afterwards and cried about it to all his friends and family. Poor, poor Haman. My guess is when Haman was answering the king's question with all the things he wanted for himself, God laughed.

CULTIVATE JOY

Picture what life would be like without laughter. How about a home without it? Boring, depressing, un-fun. If the fly on your wall could report what it hears in your home, would it include a lot of laughter? I hope when my children think back on their childhood, they remember all the giggles, jokes and comedy routines in our home. We can cultivate more joy in our families by incorporating...

A joke of the day at the dinner table

Funny Friday movie nights

Going to see a Christian comedian together

FFF...Forced Family Fun

Learn to laugh often. There is always plenty to laugh about. If we look hard enough, we can often find the humor in a situation. We must train our brains to find it, and then to laugh. Once we can snicker at happenings in the past, we can master this phrase from Proverbs 31:25: *"...she can **laugh** at the days to come."* Notice, she has no fear of the days ahead...she can "laugh." I don't know about you, but I want to be the kind of woman who can laugh at the future.

Make It Personal

1. Describe a time when God may have gotten a chuckle watching your life?

2. Do you need to look for the humorous side of a difficult situation?

3. Do you know how to use an EpiPen? If not, learn. LOL

16

A Time to Love

Love is a complex emotion. I believe God intends for love to be one of the very first emotions we feel. Most babies enter the world surrounded by people waiting to shower love on them. When I experienced the birth of my first child, Ainsley, I loved her instantly. It's fair to say I loved her before she was born, but once I had her in my arms, it felt a hundred times more powerful. The wonderful thing was, it took absolutely no effort on my part. It was easy and natural. I wish all love came that easily.

The truth is it is often much more complicated. I have three daughters, and I experienced my initial feeling of love differently with all three. It makes me wonder if God experiences love differently with each of us. When my daughter Daisy was born, the feeling of love felt blocked. Many factors were involved, but her traumatic birth definitely impacted my ability to process emotions. If you recall from the first chapter, she was born in the middle of a hurricane…literally…with no electricity or water, let alone drugs! Oh…and she was a little over nine pounds. My first thought when they placed her on me was, "She's heavy."

For the next three days, the "baby blues" hung on me like the mugginess of a hot, humid day in the South. I didn't want to experience these feelings of depression, but couldn't seem to shake them. Someone would bring this sweet, adorable baby to me, I would feed her and then ask them to take her back. I wanted to fall in love with her, but every time I looked at her, I remembered her harrowing birth. I felt desperately alone, and I couldn't tell anyone how I was feeling since it filled me with shame. On top of that, I worried whether I would ever be able to love her.

Thankfully, within the first week, my heart did start beating again with the rhythm of mother love. Even though my baby blues did not last long, I wouldn't change the experience because it fills me with more compassion for mothers who struggle with any form of post-partum depression. If you find yourself facing depression of any kind, please reach out, there are others who understand and can help. (See Appendix A.)

The unconditional love God calls us to give is a choice.

My adopted daughter, Jerilyn, was yet another type of love experience. My former husband and I adopted her when she was two-and-a-half years old. God placed her in my heart before he placed her in my home. I knew the situation she was in and was burdened to really begin praying for her, never anticipating that we might become a part of the solution. Isn't that how God often works? I fell in love with her through prayer. We adopted her and brought her home, where the real work began. She came to us with many difficult issues that I was sure love would cure. After a lot of blood, sweat and tears, she was diagnosed with autism spectrum and mood disorders.

I am not going to lie and say loving Jerilyn has always been easy, but I chose to love her a long time ago. I also choose to love her for the rest of my life—not for what she can give me, but because it is my honor and privilege. Love does not have to be a warm, fuzzy feeling all the time. No...the unconditional love that God calls us to give is a choice. It is choosing to love, without expecting anything in return. Isn't that the type of undeserved love we receive from the Father? *"But God demonstrates his own love for us in this: While we were still sinners, Christ died for us"* (Romans 5:8, NIV).

Although I cherish my initial love encounter with Ainsley, I also cherish, without reservation, my love experiences with Daisy and Jerilyn. I believe they have actually taught me more and have mined the depths of my heart to discover deeper levels of love—like precious jewels cut from the hard rocks of life, absolutely priceless treasures.

Thankfully, God doesn't wait around to love us until after we have expressed adequate amounts of love for Him. I love God with all my heart, but I still fail Him… often. The real shocker is that He knew how often I would fail Him yet still decided to offer me the best of His love. It has absolutely nothing to do with me, and everything to do with God and His choice to love me. God has *chosen* to love me!! Guess what? He has *chosen* to love *you* too!! That truth gets me excited and motivated.

Who has God placed in our lives that we need to choose to love?

A selfish husband,

critical parent,

annoying neighbor,

deceitful co-worker?

We all know someone like this. Their presence in our lives is no accident, and God obviously intends for us to learn through the relationship. We have a choice to make about whether we are going to let our relationships with them make us bitter or better. I'm not going to tell you loving that person will be easy, but it is possible, and the rewards will outweigh the effort. If it feels like a monumental task, remember what Jesus said: *"With man this is impossible, but not with God; all things are possible with God"* (Mark 10:27, NIV).

THE LINE BETWEEN LOVE AND ABUSE

If you are a woman who finds yourself trying your hardest to love a man who has passed from "difficult to love" into abusive, I would like to address your situation. It was extremely difficult for me to understand the balance between loving like 1 Corinthians 13 calls us to love and allowing someone to abuse me. The passage describes love as always patient, never keeping records of wrongs, never giving up, never losing faith, always hopeful, and enduring through every circumstance. However, the line between loving like this and enabling abusers can be very thin.

Some of us have wounds in our souls, which the enemy exploits by drawing us toward what I call the bait-and-switch relationship. We are often lured in by someone who has the traits we always wanted in a partner, only to find later that these were not true traits at all. Most women, including myself, have struggled to understand why we find ourselves in toxic relationships time and time again. We truly have a desire to love and be loved, but the object of our affection ends up becoming someone we fear. Instead of being the man who is supposed to love and protect us, he is the one from whom we need protection.

Although this is a frightening position for anyone to be in, a Christian woman often feels additional pressure that if she were to leave her abusive spouse, somehow she would be leaving Christ and walking outside of His will. She worries about the judgment within the church and her spirituality being called into question.

I want to tread lightly here, because there are multiple "right" answers in this circumstance, but they all depend on what the Holy Spirit is leading you to do. Some women stay because God has not released them, and they absolutely know God has told them not to leave. In these particular women, it is often easy to see God is carrying them through their struggle, and He is showing up in miraculous ways. I know He did that for me during the time He told me to stay.

The last year of my marriage, I spent every night on my knees praying for miracles in five areas for my husband: physical, mental, emotional, relational and spiritual. If I forgot, God would wake me up in the middle of the night to get on my knees. One night, at the exact moment I was on my knees, feeling discouraged and begging God for hope, the phone rang. My husband came in to tell me it was our next-door neighbor, inviting him to an early morning men's accountability group the following day. My hopes went up immediately. This was an answer to prayer! Satan promptly attempted to dash my hope when my husband said he wouldn't go. However, I knew God could wake him up in the morning if He wanted to, so I went to sleep peacefully. God did wake him up, and he ended up going. Did it develop into the spiritual miracle I had been praying for? No, but the evidence of God working was all around me, and that truth was what carried me through those difficult days.

Some of us have wounds in our souls, which the enemy exploits.

Other women are staying in abusive relationships because they are afraid to leave. Fear can be a harsh dictator—afraid to stay and afraid to leave. Too many of my sweet sisters are waking up with bruises, both visible and invisible, or next to a man who they know is cheating on them. The only thing holding them in the marriage is fear. God has been trying to tell them to leave. He may have used His Word, or godly counsel, or random people offering to help—yet fear holds them in place. To these women, God wants you to know He can and will take care of you.

When I left my husband, I had no money and no job. All I had was the faith to believe God was enough and that He would provide for the girls and me. He is always faithful. Let me repeat. He is *always* faithful. Although I had been looking for a job for months with no leads, I ended up with an interview the day after I left my husband. It wasn't just any interview either. Out of all the resumes I had sent out, this position was the one I wanted most of all. God not only gave me the job immediately, but He also gave me the desire of my heart. I love God. Honestly, just pondering how good God is to me brings tears of joy to my eyes.

I do understand it is hard to feel full of faith when you have been beaten down for so long. Fear and faith are polar opposites. I have made a promise to myself that if I am making a choice based on fear, I will re-evaluate it from the perspective of faith. We won't find any verse in the Bible that will back up making a decision based on fear. However, the benefits of decisions based on faith are all throughout God's Word.

Jesus loves you and values you more than you can ever imagine. You were created...by Him...His precious princess. In Luke 4:18-19, Jesus told us why He came to Earth.

The Spirit of the Lord is upon me,

for he has anointed me to bring Good News to the poor.

He has sent me to proclaim that captives will be released,

that the blind will see,

that the oppressed will be set free,

and that the time of the Lord's favor has come.

Can you relate to the captive? The blind? The oppressed? I could when I was living in abuse. Jesus set me free, and whom the Son sets free is free indeed!

If the Holy Spirit has made it clear to you to leave, don't let fear stop you. It is time to *love yourself* enough to understand the value God places on you and to *love God* enough to trust Him with your future.

Make It Personal

1. If you have children, did you experience initial love the same way with each one?

2. Do you know anyone who may be struggling with post-partum depression? If so, pray for her and see if there is any way you can offer a helping hand.

3. Are you in an abusive relationship? Pray fiercely and throw yourself into God's Word so you have clear direction. Once you have it, be obedient.

17

A Time to Mend

For a long time I believed I'd dodged the bullet on enduring the classic "broken heart." My perspective has changed now. Although I may not relate to the tale of the perfect boy who leaves and breaks your heart, during the nine years of my marriage my heart was broken piece by piece along the way.

When my dreams were laughed at,

When I was rejected time and time again,

When I kept sacrificing parts of me to keep the "false" peace.

When my marriage ended, the biggest emotion I felt was relief. It surprised me. It didn't make sense. I had loved my husband…why wasn't my heart broken? Since then, I have learned relief is actually a common response when an abusive relationship ends, for obvious reasons.

Don't misunderstand me. I was still depressed and had trouble getting out of bed and focusing on the tasks in front of me. However, whenever I thought of feeling truly heartbroken, I imagined it would consist of such deep sadness that it would change me forever.

Little did I know, my biggest heartbreak was yet to come, and it wasn't over a man. The year following my divorce, one of my daughters was a victim of abuse. It was faith-shattering for me. The overwhelming and relentless thought pursuing me every day was how God had let me down. Didn't His Word promise protection? I trusted Him to take care of my girls when I couldn't. He allowed it. He could have prevented it, and He didn't. Why?

My heart was broken into a million pieces. God has always been the one I loved most, so the fact that I hurt the most when my feelings were telling me He had abandoned me made sense. I entered into a severe crisis of faith. If God was going to allow my children to be hurt on His watch, did I really want to love Him?

My whole worldview was on the line. If I decided to blame God and distance myself from Him because He didn't meet my expectations, the foundational concepts my life was built upon would no longer exist. April, at least the April everyone knew, would also cease to exist, since my relationship with God affected every area of my life.

I felt angry, hurt and betrayed. I was being forced to answer the biggest questions of my life...would I love God even though He allowed this to happen to my little girl? Would I still trust Him, even when understanding seemed impossible?

The overwhelming and relentless thought pursuing me every day was how God had let me down.

If my answer was no, it would mean my foundation would crumble beneath me. If my answer was yes, I would have to dig deeper than ever before and choose to love God despite any circumstances He allowed or would allow in my life. I'd like to say this was a quick answer for me, but it wasn't. In the end, I chose to believe that God was all the things I knew Him to be—loving, merciful, able to make *all* things work according to His purpose, and that His will was good, pleasing and perfect. I chose God in the face of pain because my life is merely an offering unto Him. I am not here on this earth for my glory; I was created for His glory.

God doesn't report to me. He doesn't owe me any explanation. His ways are not my ways. The verse that often went through my mind was, *"Though He slay me, yet will I trust in Him"* (Job 13:15, KJV).

My heart had been broken and bruised, but it would also be mended; and although mending and healing are similar, there is a difference. Remember how our moms used to mend our jeans by sewing a patch on them? The jeans would forever look different…the patch was noticeable, but the jeans were whole again. I see mending as God stitching the pieces back together…although the evidence of our brokenness may still be apparent, it is what gives us our unique, God-designed purpose. Mending can be a painfully slow process, but we can trust God knows exactly how He is going to put the pieces back together, and His work is always perfect. When brokenness comes, and it will, my prayer is, "Lord, mend me." I then pick up the pieces of my heart and offer them back to Him, and He accepts me in my brokenness, the same way He is eager to accept all of us.

It wasn't until I decided to stop blaming God for what one person chose to do that I could start to rebuild my relationship with Him.

If we find ourselves in a place of brokenness and desperate for answers about how to move on, we must fight any desire to run from God and instead be really honest with Him. He can take it. There were times I screamed at Him, placing all blame on Him, and He still loved me. There were other times when I just cried on the floor in my feeble attempts to pray any words at all.

It wasn't until I decided to stop blaming God for what one person chose to do that I could start to rebuild my relationship with Him. I had to choose to believe God's Word even when my feelings wanted to lead me down a dark path. I had to begin looking for the ways God was bringing good out of the worst of times. Make a list, or better yet, ask a friend to make it with you. The battle is in our thoughts and minds. It's important to fill our heads and hearts with the truths of God. Listen to the Bible at night, play Christian music in the car, read the Psalms and see David cry out to God with every emotion you have experienced. David was real with God, and he was called a man after God's own heart. God wants you to be real with Him too. Trust that our God is a God of miracles.

WHO GETS THE SPICES?

My best friend, Misty, and her husband Fred got married when they were eighteen and fresh out of high school. When I met them, they were in their mid-twenties. Six years into their marriage, their relationship started falling apart, and they were on the verge of divorce.

After an initial reaction of giving up, Misty took to her knees and began praying. God started revealing what she needed to change and gave her a new understanding about her worth. Her worth came from knowing she was a child of a mighty God; it wasn't based on what her husband thought. Right before our eyes, I saw Misty become the wife God wanted her to be all along. She couldn't change Fred, but she could change herself.

God started to put Misty's broken pieces back together again. Although we had spent many hours on our knees begging for God to intervene and change the outcome, we still found ourselves packing up moving boxes, labeling some *Misty*, some *Fred*. The air was heavy with disappointment. While packing up the kitchen, I had to ask Misty whose box to put items in. When I got to the spices, I asked, "Who gets the spices?" She responded with a despondent sigh and told me, "Just give them to Fred." All of a sudden, he was taking too much from my friend, even though he wasn't even choosing them. My exact words were to her, "Heck, no, these are expensive. They are going in yours." Our laughter broke the tension of what was shaping up to be a horrible day. Fred's box *may* have included half eaten cereal containers and expired goods, but what can I say? My loyalties were a little biased.

While we were packing, Fred was forced into attending a Promise Keepers men's conference against his will, for the sole reason that some men had agreed to help him move the heavy items if he went with them. God had other plans though, which ended with Fred being heavily convicted and arriving at the door on his knees, begging for forgiveness and another chance in his marriage.

At the beginning of the day, we were set to move their stuff to two separate apartments, but by the end, we moved everything into one for a fresh start for the couple. They recently celebrated their 20th anniversary with their four beautiful children. Not only did God mend their relationship all those years ago, He blessed them exponentially. He can do the same for you.

A BROKEN PROMISE

Peter was Jesus' right-hand man; he had the faith to step out on stormy waves, the boldness to proclaim Jesus as the Son of God, and the passion to follow Jesus wherever He went. None of us is perfect, and neither was Peter. He often put his foot in his mouth, but I'm sure his most disappointing moments happened in the hours leading up to Jesus' crucifixion.

The evening of Jesus' arrest, after Peter claimed total allegiance to his Messiah, Jesus said, *"I tell you the truth, Peter—this very night, before the rooster crows twice, you will deny three times that you even know me"* (Mark 14:30).

Jesus then took Peter, James and John with Him to the Garden of Gethsemane. I imagine Jesus was at the lowest point of His life emotionally when He said, *"My soul is crushed with grief to the point of death. Stay here and keep watch with me"* (Matthew 26:38). He asked Peter, one of His best friends, to keep watch, and yet every time Jesus came to check, He found Peter asleep. How heartbreaking this must have been for Him.

It wasn't long after Judas came, betraying Jesus with a kiss, that the rest of the night begins unfolding.

So they [leading priests] arrested him [Jesus] and led him to the high priest's home. And Peter followed at a distance. The guards lit a fire in the middle of the courtyard and sat around it, and Peter joined them there. A servant girl noticed him in the firelight and began staring at him. Finally she said, "This man was one of Jesus' followers!" But Peter denied it. "Woman," he said, "I don't even know him!"

After a while someone else looked at him and said, "You must be one of them!"

"No, man, I'm not!" Peter retorted.

About an hour later someone else insisted, "This must be one of them, because he is a Galilean, too."

But Peter said, "Man, I don't know what you are talking about." And immediately, while he was still speaking, the rooster crowed.

At that moment the Lord turned and looked at Peter. Suddenly, the Lord's words flashed through Peter's mind: "Before the rooster crows tomorrow morning, you will deny three times that you even know me." And Peter left the courtyard, weeping bitterly (Luke 22: 54-62).

Peter wept bitterly because, even with the best of intentions, he had let down his best friend, his Lord. He had broken his promise to Jesus in the hour when Jesus needed him most. Two thoughts occurred to me after studying this passage. First, Jesus understands when friends let us down. Second, Peter was ashamed, full of remorse, and most likely thinking his relationship with Jesus would never be the same again.

Breaking a promise to a friend can have lasting consequences. It can change the dynamics of the relationship, create long-term trust issues, or even destroy the friendship. Thankfully, Jesus is the mender of all brokenness. After Jesus rose from the grave, He sought out Peter.

He asked Peter three times, "Do you love Me?" The original text is written in Greek, and the first two times Jesus uses the word *love* it is the Greek word *agapas,* commonly referred to as *agape.* Agape denotes unconditional love. In Peter's first two responses, he uses the word *philō* for love, which means "having an affection for" or "brotherly love." When you consider the usage of the Greek terms, the passage takes on a whole new meaning.

> *Jesus asked Simon Peter, "Simon son of John, do you agapas [unconditionally love] me more than these?"*
>
> *"Yes, Lord," Peter replied, "you know I philō [have affection for] you."*
>
> *"Then feed my lambs," Jesus told him.*
>
> *Jesus repeated the question: "Simon son of John, do you agapas [unconditionally love] me?"*
>
> *"Yes, Lord," Peter said, "you know I philō [have affection for] you."*
>
> *"Then take care of my sheep," Jesus said.*
>
> *A third time he asked him, "Simon son of John, do you philō [have affection for] me?"*
>
> *Peter was hurt that Jesus asked the question a third time. He said, "Lord, you know everything. You know that I philō [have affection for] you."*
>
> *Jesus said, "Then feed my sheep" (John 21: 15-17).*

Before Peter's denial of Jesus, he had boasted, "*Even if everyone else deserts you, I never will*" (Mark 14:29). My guess is, if Jesus had asked Peter at that time, "Do you agapas Me more than these?" Peter would have responded with a resounding "Yes." In light of his recent failure, you can see Peter struggles with confidence in his relationship with Jesus.

When I fail Jesus, I often retreat out of shame. Thankfully, we don't have a Savior who ceases to rescue us, time and time again, even from ourselves. He didn't leave Peter feeling like a failure. When Peter couldn't rise to the occasion and commit to agape Jesus, instead Jesus changed his question. He met Peter where he was and encouraged him to love again, bestowing on him the important task of ministering to others. Jesus took the time to mend the relationship between Peter and Himself because He longs for close fellowship with His children and is often willing to take the first step towards reconciliation. Don't let regret ruin your relationship with Jesus. Run to Him.

Jesus is still in the process of mending my brokenness. I see the unexpected ways He has ministered to my heart by being the husband I have always needed, providing for me without making me feel indebted to Him, and bringing friends into my life to fill in the missing gaps in my parenting. I may look like a patchwork quilt when I get to heaven, but I choose to submit myself to be mended by the Master. Join me. Let it be our Time to Mend.

Make It Personal

1. Recall times when your heart was broken. Have you allowed God to help mend your brokenness?

2. Is there someone you need to reconcile with? Are you willing to take the first step?

3. How do we deny Christ today?

4. If Jesus asked you, *"Do you agapas Me?"* what would your answer be?

18

A Time for Peace

You will keep in perfect peace all who trust in you, all whose thoughts are fixed on you! (Isaiah 26:3)

God says He will keep us in perfect peace. Perfect. Peace.

When I picture God keeping me in perfect peace, I visualize myself sitting next to my Abba Father on a porch swing, calmly swaying back and forth while in the eye of a hurricane. I hear the wind blowing, I see the leaves whipping around, but my heart is calm as we swing. I know...just *know*...everything will be fine.

Peace is made perfect when it occurs regardless of life's circumstances. In one of the bigger storms of my life, I felt like David, hiding from Saul, fearful for my safety and, even more, for the safety of my daughters. Trusting God with my own life proved challenging, but possible; trusting Him with the lives of my daughters required me to up my game and take on a whole new level of what I will affectionately call all-out-crazy faith.

At times, I was legally forced to leave my children in the care of someone who was capable of abuse. It felt similar to placing my children on the altar, walking away and hoping they would not get burned, even though the enemy stood ready with a match. These were emotionally trying times, and without God and His ability to give perfect peace, I'm not sure how I would have made it.

Fear and terror attempt to overtake me when I am facing scary obstacles, but the powerful prayers of saints have often turned the tide for me. I have learned to be at peace, not because the storm has stopped raging or the danger has passed, but because I can feel God holding me close. He is always with me, and He is with my daughters, and that is enough. Actually it is more than enough. It is everything.

I am not guaranteed a peaceful life, and neither are you, by the way, but we are guaranteed that our Father will keep us in perfect peace, even while the storm is raging around us.

PEACEMAKER VS. PEACEKEEPER

Over the years, I have completed many of Beth Moore's Bible studies, and I thank God for her inspired teaching. One of the more poignant lessons I learned from her studies has been on the topic of being a peacemaker instead of a peacekeeper. For years, I presumed myself to be a peacemaker, but in actuality, I was a peacekeeper. Allow me to explain the difference.

A peacemaker is someone who creates real and lasting peace by addressing an issue with honesty and wisdom. Peacemaking finds solutions to conflicts and creates change. Peacekeeping is when you put a bandage on a real problem using techniques like avoidance in order to create a false sense of peace. Peacekeeping creates temporal and conditional peace.

Understanding these differences led me to evaluate my relationships and how I was maintaining them. It took me quite a while to discover healthy conflict is meant to bring about change, hopefully for the better, but at the very least it allows us to be authentic and be heard. I found my most difficult and least fulfilling relationships involve me playing the role of peacekeeper. However, instead of this being my primary mode, it is now only acquiesced to when I have made multiple attempts at true peacemaking and discovered the other party is unwilling to resolve the issues. It saddens me at that point, because I realize I don't feel truly connected to the person anymore. Instead of addressing conflict, it is avoided, and I find it hard to maintain hope for the relationship.

Peacemaking should be ingrained in us from an early age so it can become our main motivation when facing conflict. One example of how to do this would be when our children are fighting, instead of sending them to opposite sides of the house and teaching them to avoid each other, we sit them down and figure out a solution, such as having them sign a contract committing to certain behaviors or actions within their relationship. When those behaviors or actions replace the fighting, you have accomplished true peacemaking.

PASSING ON

I have a friend, Mark, who was diagnosed with cancer at the young age of eighteen. He was newly married, in the military, and stationed away from family. He and his wife were a part of our Young Marrieds group at church. As we visited him in the hospital while he was undergoing a bone marrow transplant, we had the opportunity to get to know his roommate, Bertine. Bertine was also young and facing a life-threatening illness.

Bertine had a Mormon background, which prompted me to study Mormonism. My heart was heavy for him as I came to understand the differences between his religion and my Christian belief that salvation comes through faith in Jesus Christ alone.

One night, I was awakened with an intense desire to pray for Bertine. Feeling the Holy Spirit prompting me to intercede for him, I began praying for him to turn his life over to Jesus. Bertine had recently slipped into a coma, but I felt the Holy Spirit telling me, even when no one else could reach Bertine, He still could. As I interceded, a heaviness flooded my heart. I sensed this was his last opportunity to choose Jesus. My prayers became fervent. Then, all at once, an overwhelming peace descended upon me and, in my heart, I knew Bertine had passed from this life to eternity with our Lord. Not surprisingly, when speaking with Mark later, I learned Bertine had passed away during the time I was praying. I look forward to rejoicing in heaven together, knowing our Father never gives up on us and connects believers in a way that passes understanding.

PEACE THAT PASSES UNDERSTANDING

Have you ever experienced the peace that passes understanding? In my life, it occurs during times when circumstances are so difficult that peace is the last thing you expect. It happens when family and friends not only expect you to worry, but do so for you as well. Peace seems impossible, and yet, we all can experience it, even during...

The sudden death of a loved one.

A shattering medical diagnosis for a family member.

The loss of a career.

A terrorist attack.

A false accusation.

Although our world may be rocked, God is not surprised. Better than that, He has a special gift in store for us—peace. He offers peace that flows like a river, not peace that sits stagnant like a lake. (See Isaiah 66:12.) No, peace flows over us, purifying us of all our worries. Just like a river wears down the rocks until they are smooth and no longer a hindrance, peace flows over our worries or concerns until they are pebbles and not big boulders in our path.

This peace becomes a powerful witness to those watching us as we endure the trial, it will leave many amazed at how we are handling everything. The truth is, God is handling everything, which is why we can accept the peace He offers. Just like the childhood hymn, *He's Got the Whole World in His Hands*, the only way to peace that passes understanding is through faith in a God who has our whole world in His hands.

An inspiring example of a peace that passes understanding is found in Horatio Spafford, the author of the hymn "It Is Well With My Soul." The Great Chicago Fire of 1871 hit Horatio particularly hard financially. He was a lawyer but had invested heavily into real estate before most of the city burned down in the fire. In 1873, he was scheduled to leave with his family on a trip to Europe and at the last minute had to stay behind for a business emergency.

The ship carrying his wife and four daughters left. While in the middle of the Atlantic, their ship was struck by a British iron sailing ship and quickly sank. Anna, Horatio's wife, survived and sent the following cable to him, "Saved alone. What should I do..."All four of their daughters had perished. Having three daughters of my own, I can't imagine the utter horror and devastation he and his wife felt.

Peace becomes a powerful witness to those watching us as we endure the trial.

Horatio immediately left to be by her side. The captain of the ship on which he was sailing called Horatio to the bridge as they passed over the spot where the shipwreck occurred. Later that night, in his room, Horatio penned the words to the famous and inspiring hymn "It Is Well With My Soul." Read these words and let Horatio's wisdom in the face of great loss allow God to bring you the peace that passes understanding.

It Is Well With My Soul

(Original lyrics by Horatio Spafford)

When peace like a river, attendeth
my way,
When sorrows like sea billows
roll;
Whatever my lot, Thou hast
taught me to *know,*[a]
It is well, it is well, with my soul.

It is well, (it is well),
With my soul, (with my soul)
It is well, it is well, with my soul.

Though Satan should buffet,
though trials should come,
Let this blest assurance control,
That Christ has regarded my
helpless estate,
And hath shed His own blood for
my soul.

My sin, oh, the bliss of this
glorious thought!
My sin, not in part but the whole,
Is nailed to the cross, and I bear it
no more,
Praise the Lord, praise the Lord, O
my soul!

For me, be it Christ, be it Christ
hence to live:
If Jordan above me shall roll,
No pang shall be mine, for in
death as in life,
Thou wilt whisper Thy peace to
my soul.

But Lord, 'tis for Thee, for Thy
coming we wait,
The sky, not the grave, is our goal;
Oh, trump of the angel! Oh, voice
of the Lord!
Blessed hope, blessed rest of my
soul.

And Lord, haste the day when my
faith shall be sight,
The clouds be rolled back as a
scroll;
The trump shall resound, and the
Lord shall descend,
A song in the night, oh my soul! [b]

[a] "know" (at the end of the third line) was
changed to "say"
[b] "A song in the night, oh my soul" (last line)
was changed to "Even so, it is well with my
soul."

Make It Personal

1. What do you envision when you think of "perfect peace?"

2. Do you think you are more often a peacemaker or a peacekeeper? Give examples of both in your life.

3. In what circumstance do you need peace right now? Ask God to supply it.

19

A Time to Plant

As far as planting goes, I have a black thumb. Plants usually come to me to die. It's not pretty. Fortunately, I am not responsible for growing my own food, otherwise my children would have no doubt starved. However, I am responsible for planting a different kind of seed, not only into my own soul, but into the lives of my children, friends and whoever else God puts in front of me.

When we keep ourselves open to God's plan, He asks us to plant seeds; and those seeds are often truths from His Word. I have found planting God's Word in my heart is vital for me in my many roles as….

Woman

Mother

Friend

Christian

Often God will bring a Scripture to mind, buried there years ago. He wants me to apply knowledge to the situation or circumstance before me. For instance, one time I was traveling to speak at a conference, and when I arrived in the airport, the terminal was extremely crowded. I ended up sitting next to a young lady busy studying her Bible. I started a conversation with her, only to discover she was at a crossroads in her life. She had recently become a Christian and was faced with a difficult decision requiring her to put her faith into practice and alter her current course.

God planted me there, in that terminal, in that seat, in order to speak God's Word into her life. He brought multiple Scriptures to mind that I was able to share with her, encouraging her in the step of faith she was making. God's Spirit was right there with us. In fact, we were so engrossed with our conversation, everyone else had already boarded before we realized we were about to miss the plane if we didn't go.

The fact is God can use anyone to get a message to one of His children. We make ourselves open and ready to be used by Him when we plant His word in our hearts. He tells us His word will never return void (Isaiah 55:11). He will use the time and energy we invest in His word, and one day we will help reap the harvest.

A PARENT'S GOTTA PLANT

Parenting is, by far, the biggest planting gig I've ever had. Not only are we responsible for planting spiritual understanding, but also love, joy, peace, patience, kindness, goodness, faithfulness, gentleness and self-control. I can't possibly plant these things into my children's lives if I am incapable of growing them in my own life.

Thankfully, I have a friend, Maureen, whose special gift is fabulous parenting. She is one of those women born to be a mom. The role fits her perfectly, and she is always the one I run to for advice. She keeps me accountable to planting the fruit of the Spirit into my children.

Maureen inspires me to plant spiritual disciplines into my daughters as I've seen her consistently praying over and with her children. The faithfulness she and her husband have demonstrated has included bringing other children desperate for love into their home. These children are inevitably introduced to the perfect Father—God—and their lives are changed for eternity.

BLOOM WHERE YOU ARE PLANTED

Bloom where you are planted! I love that phrase, especially since I believe it directly applies to my life.

I moved seven times in nine years of marriage. When you move as much as we did, you start to develop a system. Usually, my then husband would get offered a promotion and be gone in a matter of days, off to the new city, leaving me to get our house ready to place on the market…which is especially fun with a couple of preschoolers running around, destroying the room I just cleaned.

As I began getting our house ready to sell, I would also have to make trips to the new location to house hunt for our next home. Usually that meant long drives at night, hoping and praying the girls would sleep, and that I wouldn't have to get gas or go to the bathroom…because as soon as the car stopped moving, they would inevitably wake up again.

I like change, honestly I do. I was on board for all of our moves. However, one of those was across the country, from Washington State to Tampa, Florida. The cross-country move took a toll on me. I was pregnant with my daughter Daisy, still in the first trimester, and exhausted all the time. By the time we arrived in Tampa, I was ready to call it quits on the moves. We would just live in Tampa forever and that was that.

Another thing I came to expect was my emotional breakdown, which would occur about six weeks into our new place. You could practically set your clock by it. I am an extreme people person. Six weeks after moving to a new place was when it would click—*I'm lonely.* Trying to stay connected to my long-distance friends by talking on the phone wasn't the same. Their lives were going on without me, and I felt like I didn't belong anywhere. After a good cry, I would decide to dry my tears and find some new friends.

The most logical place for me to make new connections was the church. I would start church shopping in our new city, look for a Bible study group to get involved in and simply force them to be my new friends! I actually met many good, godly women this way—friends I still have to this day. However, my plan didn't work in Tampa. We found a church quickly and joined a class with couples our age, but we didn't seem to click with anybody. This was new territory for me, and I didn't have a backup plan.

God plants us where He can grow and stretch us.

After talking to my dad on the phone one night, he reminded me of something he told me right before we made the move to Tampa. He felt like the Lord impressed upon him that I was moving to Tampa to reach the lost for Christ. I believe my initial reaction was, "Excuse me…evangelize? You must have heard Him wrong, Dad." I am not going to deny God is able to do anything He wants through His believers, but I could not fathom *evangelizing* would be something God would ask of me. Since then I have come to realize God plants us where He can grow and stretch us. Think about it…we don't plant an oak tree in a tiny pot, hoping it never outgrows it, do we? Well, neither does God. Sometimes He transplants us to a new area where we can grow without our former limitations. It feels uncomfortable at the time, but He understands much better than we do how much room we need to grow during our next season.

I had always cocooned myself in Christian circles where I felt safe. No one challenged my beliefs. All of my friends operated under virtually the same worldview. Our foundations were the same. I convinced myself God was happy enough with me teaching ladies' Bible studies and involving myself with church ministries. He didn't need me to go out there and win souls…that was better suited to other people.

When my plan to find new friends in church fell through, I was forced to look around me and see where else I might be able to make those connections. I decided my neighbors would be my first targets. The problem was, it didn't appear we had chosen a "friendly" type of neighborhood. When people came home, they would open the garage door, drive in and close it behind them. All of the backyards were fenced, and although I could hear children playing, we never actually saw them.

I was on a mission. I told the girls, "Prepare to play in the front yard today." I pulled out a chair, plopped it on the driveway and waited for my targets, I mean neighbors. As soon as they came home, I sent the girls their way and pulled them into conversations. Amazingly, it didn't take long for people to start to warm up…I mean, my girls *were* adorable! We began making friends, and soon more and more neighbors joined us on our afternoon stakeouts. I was able to connect with some of the ladies, none of whom attended church, I might add.

My dad had been right. God had plans to expand the boundaries I had placed on my abilities and use me in a new way. I felt very humbled and found a new boldness in my faith. God allowed me many opportunities to not only tell those women about God's love for them, but also actually show them with my actions.

Nine months into living there, after I had vowed this was the last move I could make, my former husband took another transfer. We were moving again. I was disappointed, but I knew God had fulfilled his purpose for me there. I was able to encourage one woman who had walked away from her faith to turn back to God, to boldly give the plan of salvation to a woman who grew up in a cult but was now seeking the truth, and to have the awesome privilege of leading another woman into a relationship with the Lord.

I cherish the time I lived there and the lessons God taught me. I stopped trusting in my abilities and learned to depend on God to use me despite my weaknesses. Thank goodness God doesn't leave us trapped in our comfort zones. He is in the business of stretching us, showing His Word to be true. *"For when I am weak, then I am strong"* (2 Corinthians 12:10). My prayer now is that I will always be open to wherever God wants to plant me.

Is there anything you have ever told God or others you couldn't do? Do yourself a favor and don't limit God's ability to do ANYTHING through you. In God's economy, the blessings of obedience always outweigh the imagined costs.

Make It Personal

1. Is planting God's Word in your heart a priority? If not, how can you make it one?

2. Which fruit of the Holy Spirit (love, joy, peace, patience, kindness, goodness, faithfulness, or self-control) do you see growing strongest in your life? Which fruit needs more planting in your heart?

3. Have you been planted anywhere outside of your comfort zone? What can you learn from the experience?

20

A Time to Be Quiet

Have you ever been to the Vatican and seen Michelangelo's Sistine Chapel? I was blessed to be able to visit Rome one year in August, and for those of you who don't know, or perhaps live under a rock, Italy is predominately Catholic. The Vatican being there kind of gives it away.

What I *didn't* know is that the Assumption of the Virgin Mary on August 15 is apparently a pretty darn big holiday to Catholics, especially Italian Catholics. In fact, most businesses close down for up to two weeks surrounding it, and most of those who live in the city leave for vacation. This created quite the challenge in finding open restaurants and attractions. When the Vatican reopened on the sixteenth, we were some of the first to gain entrance amidst throngs of tourists.

We walked straight to the Sistine Chapel. Can I just say…gorgeous! Pictures don't do it justice. In fact, it is so beautiful and awe-inspiring, your soul understands at once that it is *a time to be quiet*. It was silent when we arrived in the first group, before the room was packed wall to wall with people, but even as the room quickly filled to capacity, it seemed everyone felt the same need to be reverently quiet.

I didn't want to leave; I wanted to dwell in this place of quiet, soaking in the man-made, but obviously God-inspired, work of art. It is the same feeling I get as I...

> sit to watch a sunrise or sunset,
>> gaze at the glorious stars, or
>>> watch the waves pound the seashore.

I see God's artwork all over nature. His absolute brilliance and power, especially in creation, gives me a deep desire to be quiet in His presence.

Quiet comes only after I have finally ceased talking. Yes...*finally*. I wonder if God sometimes creates a beautiful sunset just to shut me up for a few minutes. I'm okay with it if He does.

SILENCE BEFORE THE SHOUT

When Joshua led the Israelites in The Battle of Jericho, the Prince of the LORD, whom many believe was Jesus himself, came to Joshua with specific instructions. Joshua relayed these instructions to his army.

> *"Do not shout; do not even talk," Joshua commanded. "Not a single word from any of you until I tell you to shout. Then shout!" (Joshua 6:10)*

For six days the army marched around the entire city of Jericho in complete silence—total quiet. I wonder what the people of Jericho thought?

What are they doing?

> *Don't you think it's strange they aren't saying anything?*
>> *What's that big box they are carrying around?*
>>> *Why don't they just go ahead already?*
>>>> *They really don't think there is even a slight chance they can get through our wall, do they?*

As the Israelite army silently marched around the walls, the questions and rumors must have been building to a crescendo within the walls. There is power in silence though, power in the quiet eye of a hurricane. The Israelites were obedient, and when they finished the last lap on the seventh day the *time to be quiet* ended with a loud shout. Their obedience allowed God's power to be revealed in an earth-shaking way, as the walls came tumbling down. There is a time to be quiet and a time to shout; as we walk in the Holy Spirit's power, He will lead us to understand the difference.

GENTLE AND QUIET

Every woman wants to be beautiful. Isn't it a relief to know true beauty is not based on our outward appearance, which is fleeting? Our beauty is based on cultivating a gentle and quiet spirit.

> *"You should clothe yourselves instead with the beauty that comes from within, the unfading beauty of a gentle and quiet spirit, which is so precious to God" (1 Peter 3:4).*

Don't fall for the lie Satan has been promoting for the last fifty years in our country. Beauty is not a synonym for young, thin, skinny, toned or in shape. Beauty is deeper than this world's definition.

Admittedly, it is one thing to know this in my head and another thing to convince myself when I am standing in front of a mirror feeling inadequate, overweight and *not* beautiful. As a young woman, I could eat whatever I wanted and exercise as little as I desired with absolutely no change to my body. Now I find myself avoiding taking pictures because I don't like how I look.

Self-image is a fragile thing. One thing I know for sure is that I will not be telling my sweet heavenly Father that He missed the mark when He made my body....He did create this outer shell, didn't He? The other thing I know is that He has not hidden the truth of how we obtain "unfading beauty."

God's Word speaks to women specifically on having a quiet spirit. No one ever seems to ask why God didn't tell men to have a quiet spirit...then again, I think it's pretty obvious once you know the facts. Studies show women speak about 20,000 words a day while men make it to a whopping 7,000. Apparently, we talk almost three times as much as they do. I'm guessing it is because we are forced to repeat ourselves since our families never "hear" us the first time! Well, that, and the fact we are just slam-bam awesome girlfriends who actually share with each other what goes on in our lives.

Beauty is not a synonym for young, thin, skinny, toned or in shape. Beauty is deeper than this world's definition.

God planted the strong desire to communicate within us as women, and I believe it is a strength; however, we still need to exert control over this area of our lives. God tells us to have a *gentle and quiet spirit* because it is precious to Him. I really want to be precious to Him, and if that means cultivating a quiet spirit, I'm willing.

The Bible lists only two instances where the phrase *precious to God* is used. The first is when the angel appears to Daniel with a message from God, telling him he is very precious to Him (Daniel 10:11). The other is in the verse above, 1 Peter 3:4. As women, God has given us the opportunity to be *precious* to Him. Let's not squander the opportunity, but instead work diligently to be just that.

Here are some ways we can work on our preciousness:

- Set aside time to be alone with God, even if it means hiding in the closet or the bathroom. For some moms, this is the only quiet place they can find!
- Practice the art of listening to others. Stop interrupting others and listen in an attempt to *understand* instead of waiting only for the next pause so we can jump in and contribute to the conversation.

- Take a moment to stop and smell the roses, take in a sunset or gaze at the stars.
- Practice taking deep breaths when our children whine. This one used to set me on edge and, instead of having a *gentle and quiet* spirit, I often ended up with a harsh and loud spirit.
- Seek wise counsel. Approach other women whom we can see have already mastered this ability and ask them to come alongside and help us learn.

I admit the hardest time for me to be quiet is when I am ready for a fight, usually with my family. Choosing humility over the desire to prove my case is a challenge for a bossy pants like me. Left to our own natural inclination, I would bet most of us stop listening during an argument. We see our opposition's mouth moving, but we are too busy thinking of what we will say next to actually listen to them.

However, I have also noticed that when I do focus on staying quiet, listening allows me to live out the verse, *"You must all be quick to listen, slow to speak, and slow to get angry"* (James 1:19). The disagreement tends to have a better result. Following God's Word will not leave us feeling weak; instead, the strength it takes to stop the constant flow of words and heavy emotions will strengthen us. I find that it gets easier and easier the more I put it into practice.

Sometimes silence…

...is exactly…

...what is needed.

LISTEN FOR THE WHISPER

"Go out and stand before me on the mountain," the Lord told him. And as Elijah stood there, the Lord passed by, and a mighty windstorm hit the mountain. It was such a terrible blast that the rocks were torn loose, but the Lord was not in the wind. After the wind there was an earthquake, but the Lord was not in the earthquake. And after the earthquake there was a fire, but the Lord was not in the fire. And after the fire there was the sound of a gentle whisper. When Elijah heard it, he wrapped his face in his cloak and went out and stood at the entrance of the cave (1 Kings 19:11-13).

I find it poignant that God used the whisper to speak to Elijah. Often we are so distracted by the volatile circumstances of life, we have to be reminded to listen for the whisper.

It is easy to focus on the storm that is ripping apart our life, but if we want to hear God's voice, we need to be still and quiet. The irony is, when life is crazy and chaotic and quiet is nearly impossible, that is when it is most vital for us to hear God's voice calming and clarifying His will for us.

BITING MY TONGUE

My girlfriend came to me and shared some of her recent struggles, and although they brought her to tears, all I could think was **if only** *those were my problems.* It's easy for many of us who have been weathering serious storms in our lives for months or years to have an attitude of pride in our pain. It's not that we like or even want the pain, but we do begin to feel like the depths of our struggles somehow make us more worthy. I find myself wanting to drop a few bombshells on others to rock their world about how tough life can really be, but what kind of friend does that make me? Obviously, not a friend at all. *"A friend loves at all times"* (Proverbs 17:17). Since we know love is kind, not proud, and not self-seeking (1 Corinthians 13:4-5), it is clear one-upping the other person is just not a friendly thing to do. It means listening….quietly, without having it be about us or our story. We are not in a contest for the winner of the worst life, because, believe me, no one wins.

When divorced and co-parenting with a former spouse, there are many, many times when we need to be quiet in front of our children. Believe me, I understand this can be a real challenge. It is tough to balance telling your kids the truths they need to know and not telling them the truths they don't need to know. My policy is to err on the side of not telling them, trusting the truth will win out in the end. When my children are grown, I don't want them remembering me always talking down about their father.

When my children bring up all the luxury items he owns, I bite my tongue instead of saying anything about him not paying child support. When they report to me the damaging ways he talks about me, I trust they cling to the real truth.

The truth is, my children learn more about me when I choose to be quiet. They learn I am not on a mission to destroy their current view of him. They learn how to choose the moral high road. They learn to let actions speak louder than words.

Many lessons in life can be learned in the silence…by all of us.

Make It Personal

1. Where is the best place for you to go to find quiet?

2. Who around you exemplifies a gentle and quiet spirit? What can you learn from them?

3. Challenge yourself to be a listener in the next disagreement you have, whether it be with a co-worker, friend or spouse.

21

A Time to Quit Searching

In between finishing junior college and starting at my university, I needed a full-time summer job. After running into a lot of dead ends, I decided to quit searching on my own and headed to an employment agency. They sent me out on my first job as a receptionist for a door and hardware company. Now, I knew as much about doors and hardware as I knew about rocket science—which was a big, fat zero since physics was the only class I ever ran from screaming, uh…I mean, dropped.

I was told the job would be only until the end of the week, but the company confided after a couple days that they were looking for someone to replace the current employee and would like me to take the position. I informed them I would be able to work there only until school started in the fall. They agreed and hired me.

The job turned out to be a great fit. I enjoyed being the hub for the office, putting my natural-born sarcasm to good use with the "rough around the edges," mostly male staff. As the summer neared its close, the company began asking me to stay on full time. My daily reply became, "No, thank you, I am heading to school in the fall."

Then they began adding incentives to their request. First, it was season tickets to the Seattle Seahawks games. It was obvious they didn't know me at all! Sports just don't do it for me. Next, it was season tickets to the theatre downtown. Okay…maybe they did know me a little. This one was harder to say no to, but I stuck to my mantra, "No, thank you, I am headed to school in the fall."

Last, but not least, they offered to help me pay for school. Now they had my attention! The University of Puget Sound, the private school I would be attending, was not cheap…at all. I had no idea how we would pay for it, except with a lot of loans. The company asked me to come up with a few proposals of how I could continue working there while they helped with my schooling.

I offered them three options. They ended up choosing the option where I worked about thirty hours a week, took only a $1 an hour pay cut, and they would pay $5,000 of my tuition every semester. It was a massive blessing.

Unfortunately, the company ended up closing its doors only ten months after I began working there. One of the last checks processed was the $5,000 payment for my spring semester. All in all, I received $10,000 for my schooling while still earning the income I needed. God was providing for me without a shadow of a doubt, and I was and still am completely in awe of His provision. Whenever I am stressed about jobs or money, remembering this example of God's faithfulness reminds me to stop searching for the answers in myself and trust Him to provide.

CHURCH (S)HOPPING

Sometimes what we are asking God to provide is a new church family. The process of searching for a church can be a frustrating process. The first question we should ask ourselves is whether we are church hopping or church shopping. Church hopping is when we find ourselves in a pattern of staying at a church for a short length of time before once again beginning to search for a "better" church. Church shopping takes place when we are visiting churches because God has clearly told us to leave our current church, or we are new to town or possibly *old* to town but looking to mend our "hopping" ways.

After one move, we must have tried every church within a fifteen-mile radius without getting that heaven-opening-up-and-angels-singing moment, which usually cemented that we had found the "right" church. We ended up just choosing a church and began faithfully attending and serving. No church is going to be perfect, and I guarantee that the more involved we are in serving the Lord in a church, the more we will see that all churches are run by sinners. Every. Single. One. Of. Them.

Even more shocking…not only are the churches run by sinners, but they are also attended by sinners. Gasp! We shouldn't let this fact—and it is absolutely a fact—make us perpetual church hoppers. God's Word is clear.

> *We should not stop gathering together with other believers, as some of you are doing. Instead, we must continue to encourage each other even more as we see the day of the Lord coming (Hebrews 10:25, GW).*

It's time to quit searching for the perfect church and become the best church member we can be. When we stop thinking about what we can get out of a church and start considering what we can give to the body of Christ, we will reap the blessing of obedience.

Maybe we aren't looking for the perfect church, but we may be searching for the perfect...

> Spouse,
>> Child,
>>> Home,
>>>> Job.

The endless search for perfection in others or ourselves will always leave us disappointed. Jesus was and always will be the ONLY perfect one ever. Measured against Him, we all fail miserably; but He doesn't make it His mission to focus on our failures. Instead, He offers abundant grace and never-ending encouragement. I wonder how our perspectives would change if we did the same in our relationships...purposely looking for ways to encourage others instead of focusing on how imperfect people fail us. It may not be an easy change for some of us, but usually the most difficult changes bring the greatest rewards.

WHY???

One of the most difficult challenges for me has been grappling with not finding answers to the "why" questions that come when facing trials.

Why am I going through this?

Why are my children suffering?

Why am I paying the price for someone else's sin?

Why can't I hear you, God?

Getting wrapped up in finding the answers to the "why" questions can lead to further discouragement, as though the trial were not discouraging enough. This is a trap most fall into at one time or another. We are human. We were made to question why. One needs only to hang around a three year old for a few hours to see that "why?" is the number one question of the day...every day.

However, God asks us to walk by faith, not by sight, which means we don't always have the answers to our questions. Although our flesh screams out for answers, our spirit tells us "be truly glad" regardless of whether the questions are still looming.

So be truly glad. There is wonderful joy ahead, even though you have to endure many trials for a little while (1 Peter 1:6).

"A little while" surely can seem subjective. Every family has sins that seem to appear generation after generation. My family is no different. In fact, I found one particular sin popping up over and over again as I studied our family tree. As a preemptive measure, I put safeguards in place to protect my children from encountering this issue. However, even with these in place, the sin made its way to them. My persistent question to God was, "Why? Why? Why?" His answer, even to this day on this matter, is silence.

He doesn't make it His mission to focus on our failures.

I came to the realization it was *time to quit searching* for the answer to "why" and instead rest in knowing that even if I don't understand, God does. He is able to bring good out of what I perceive as bad. His Word promises He is able to bring beauty from ashes (Isaiah 61:3). My job is to trust Him.

My story is not unique. We all have at least one unanswered "why" rattling around in our minds, and the truth is we may never know the reason we…

Suffered abuse at the hands of another…

Face failure time and time again…

Experienced the loss of a loved one too early…

Suffer physically.

I may never have the answers to all of my "why" questions, but when we quit searching for the answers, 1 Peter 1:7 becomes our blessing.

> *So be truly glad. There is wonderful joy ahead, even though you have to endure many trials for a little while. These trials will show that your faith is genuine. It is being tested as fire tests and purifies gold—though your faith is far more precious than mere gold. So when your faith remains strong through many trials, it will bring you much praise and glory and honor on the day when Jesus Christ is revealed to the whole world (1 Peter 1:6-7).*

Please understand, I'm not saying it is easy to walk away from our mantra of "why, why, why?" I'm also not undermining the importance the answers can play in bringing about spiritual healing from our pasts. However, many people have turned their backs on God because they can't accept not knowing why. We must not let our need to know trump our need for a Savior. Just cling to Him. Besides, if it is still bothering us, we can always ask Him once we get to heaven!

Make It Personal

1. What is an example in your life when God has provided in an unexpected way for you?

2. Do you find yourself prone to church hopping? Ask God to help you stay committed to a church family.

3. Do you have a "why" question that haunts you? Prayerfully ask God to release you from needing the answer and instead increase your faith in Him.

22

A Time to Scatter Stones

Jesus returned to the Mount of Olives, but early the next morning he was back again at the Temple. A crowd soon gathered, and he sat down and taught them. As he was speaking, the teachers of religious law and the Pharisees brought a woman who had been caught in the act of adultery. They put her in front of the crowd.

"Teacher," they said to Jesus, "this woman was caught in the act of adultery. The law of Moses says to stone her. What do you say?"

They were trying to trap him into saying something they could use against him, but Jesus stooped down and wrote in the dust with his finger. They kept demanding an answer, so he stood up again and said, "All right, but let the one who has never sinned throw the first stone!" Then he stooped down again and wrote in the dust.

When the accusers heard this, they slipped away one by one,

beginning with the oldest, until only Jesus was left in the middle of the crowd with the woman. Then Jesus stood up again and said to the woman, "Where are your accusers? Didn't even one of them condemn you?"

"No, Lord," she said.

And Jesus said, "Neither do I. Go and sin no more" *(John 8: 8-11).*

I hear the *thud, thud* of stones falling in sand. One of my questions for Jesus when I get to heaven is, "What did you write in the sand that day?" One minute everyone in the crowd is ready to stone the woman to death, and the next she's alone with her Savior, stones meant for harm lying scattered around her.

Have you ever committed a sin, where shame and feelings of failure made you fear God's punishment? I have. This story shows us the depths of God's love and compassion. Not only does He *not* pick up a stone, He convicts the hearts of those prideful enough to sit in judgment. The truth is, He is the only one who can rightfully judge this woman, and His verdict is grace. What an awesome Savior we have!

Jesus is NOT our accuser.

I have to rely on God's grace because sin is a common occurrence for me. An extrovert who often talks before I think, I can "throw stones" with my words in those little quips that slip out. I am instantly convicted and disappointed in myself. It reminds me of a boomerang. I throw out ugliness, and it turns around and hits me in my soul. I am grateful God is not waiting for me to fail so He can throw a stone, because I have given Him ample opportunities. Instead, He offers His grace, an undeserved gift.

God's grace can be challenging to accept when we are our own worst critics. We pick up a lot of hurts and grievances as we move through life, which can weigh down our hearts. Our inner dialogue turn out to be stones we throw at ourselves.

> I hate my body…it's disgusting.

> My husband doesn't love me.

> I am a failure.

> My children deserve a better mom.

The same Jesus who tells our accusers to drop their stones is also telling us to drop the stones we hold. His grace and mercy covered the adulterous woman that fateful day. Do not doubt that His grace and mercy is sufficient to cover you.

Jesus is NOT our accuser.

THE REAL ACCUSER

> *One day the members of the heavenly court came to present themselves before the Lord, and the Accuser, Satan, came with them (Job 1:6).*

> *For the accuser of our brothers and sisters has been thrown down to earth—the one who accuses them before our God day and night (Revelation 12:10).*

Satan is "the Accuser" from Genesis to Revelation. In fact, the very first time he speaks, he tells Eve that God has lied.

> *The serpent was the shrewdest of all the wild animals the Lord God had made. One day he asked the woman, "Did God really say you must not eat the fruit from any of the trees in the garden?"….*

> *"You won't die!" the serpent replied to the woman. "God knows that your eyes will be opened as soon as you eat it, and you will be like God, knowing both good and evil" (Genesis*

3:1, 4-5).

Satan hasn't changed. He's not busy "working on himself" or learning to abstain from past infractions. He doesn't feel guilty, and he's not holding himself accountable to a twelve-step program. Just like with the adulterous woman, he tempts us to sin and then accuses us of that sin. Guilt, self-loathing, emotional torment...these are his tools, not God's. The good news is, one day Satan will be permanently defeated.

> *Then the devil, who had deceived them, was thrown into the fiery lake of burning sulfur, joining the beast and the false prophet. There they will be tormented day and night forever and ever (Revelation 20:10).*

There is no need to wait until Satan is judged before our Almighty God. We must choose today to stop giving the Accuser our ear. This is not to say we are without sin; heaven knows that's not true. However, there is a difference between having godly sorrow, which leads to repentance, and the accusations and guilt Satan tries to pile on us.

We have to stop beating ourselves up over our sin. God knows our sin—past, present and future—and He's already chosen to put down the stones. He doesn't make mistakes. He just loves us and then loves us some more.

Drop those stones you carry...just let them fall to the ground.

STICKS AND STONES

> *Sticks and stones may break my bones,*
>
> *but words will never hurt me.*

Eventually we all realize that this childhood taunt is about as inaccurate as it gets. Words do hurt when hurled at us, and the bruises they cause can create lasting pain no one else sees.

We can learn to stop casting stones at ourselves, but we can't always stop others from throwing stones at us. No specific stone aimed at me has ever delivered a deathblow; however, the intent was often to do just that, and it resulted in internal bleeding.

Some of the stones thrown at me sounded like this...

You are worthless.

You are a liar.

You alienate the children from me.

You are lazy.

My relationship with my former husband has always been tumultuous, and he had an endless arsenal of stones to throw at me. Over time, the stones began to pile up, so I came up with the brilliant idea to use them to build a wall of protection, determined to defend my body, soul and spirit. But in my quest for protection, I built a stone wall around myself. This wall blocked me not only from my enemy but also from other relationships. It's hard to hear anyone who is trying to communicate with me when they have to yell over a ten-foot wall. I had to learn to tear down my wall and scatter those stones if I wanted to move on towards developing healthy relationships.

It wasn't easy for me. It took some heavy emotional lifting, but eventually the walls came down. Now, instead of letting stones pile up, I pick them up and immediately toss them away with truth attached.

You are worthless...   *I am a child of God (1 John 5:1).*

You are a liar...   *Silence their lying lips—those proud and arrogant lips that accuse the godly (Psalm 31:18).*

You alienate the children... *A false witness will not go unpunished, and a liar will be destroyed (Proverbs 19:9).*

You are lazy...   *Yes, just as you can identify a tree by its fruit, so you can identify people by their actions (Matthew 7:20).*

God's truth is full of power. As we embrace it, our enemy's lies fade away. The adulterous woman walked away untouched by a stone, but indelibly touched by her Savior...*our* Savior. Let His truth, grace and mercy wash over you as well.

Make It Personal

1. What stones are being thrown at you? What are your enemy's accusations? Go to the Bible and begin reading, praying, and speaking God's Word over yourself. God's Word is eternal. Your enemies and their accusations are temporal.

2. Take a few minutes to write down the accusations the enemy aims at you, then research verses to combat the lies and speak the truth over your life. Write these verses on sticky notes and scatter them throughout your home. Here are a few to get you started.

   There is therefore now no condemnation for those who are in Christ Jesus (Romans 8:1).

   I will give thanks to You, for I am fearfully and wonderfully made (Psalm 139:14a).

   Love is patient and kind. Love is not jealous or boastful or proud or rude. It does not demand its own way. It is not irritable, and it keeps no record of being wronged (1 Corinthians 13:4-5).

"For I know the plans I have for you," says the Lord. "They are plans for good and not for disaster, to give you a future and a hope" (Jeremiah 29:11).

Fill in the chart with the accusations thrown at you by others or by Satan. Then combat them with the TRUTH!

Accusations the Enemy Makes About Me	God's Truth

23

A Time to Search

Do you remember playing hide and seek as a child? When I was "it" and had to search longer than a few minutes for a playmate, I would start to lose my patience. If the search took too long, the game started to fizzle out. It's amazing how something that begins with so much fun can end in such frustration.

As newborn Christians, we are typically filled with a sense of excitement. Once lost but now found, we are filled with a desire to seek out and save the lost. It motivates us to get out there and proclaim the Good News. We have a fire underneath us, but all too often we get tired if our passion doesn't produce the quick results we want, and we let the flame die.

At first glance, searching seems like a relatively easy task, but the endurance required for the search creates the challenge. I'm sure this is why so many Scriptures in the Bible encourage us to search for the Lord. Thankfully, His Word promises that when we do search for Him, we will surely find Him.

> *I love all who love me. Those who search will surely find me*
> *(Proverbs 8:17).*

*But from there you will **search** again for the Lord your God.
And if you **search** for him with all your heart and soul, you
will find him (Deuteronomy 4:29).*

*Our God is so
merciful that,
even when we fail
to spend time
with Him, He
still pursues us.*

I hate to admit it, but I often find myself waxing
and waning in my pursuit of an intimate relationship
with God. There are times when I am on fire for Him,
learning, growing and sharing with others. Then there
are periods when I let the fire dwindle because I am
not feeding it. I skip a day or a week or more of Bible
reading and prayer. The impact on my daily life is
noticeable. I begin to realize I don't have as much
patience with my family; I lose the inner peace only
Jesus provides and start to get sucked into worry or anxiety.

Even knowing this, I find myself slipping into the habit of not pursuing
God every day. There are no excuses for, and no benefits or rewards to,
forging ahead without God. Paul's verse in Romans illustrates how I feel.

*I don't really understand myself, for I want to do what is
right, but I don't do it. Instead, I do what I hate (Romans
7:15).*

Thankfully, God keeps a short-ish leash on me, and I can't go too terribly
long without bowing my knee and confessing my rebellious heart. God has
been far too good to me for me to ignore Him. The life verse I chose for
myself a long time ago was Philippians 3:10, and I love the Amplified version
the best.

*For my determined purpose is that I may know Him that I
may progressively become more deeply and intimately
acquainted with Him, perceiving and recognizing and
understanding the wonders of His Person more strongly and
more clearly.*

If I am committed to this pursuit, it obviously requires consistently acknowledging God. As Christians we have all been called to steadfastly seek God, and it requires endurance on days when we don't feel like doing so. We must also learn that no matter how far we have strayed, Jesus is waiting with open arms as soon as we turn towards Him again.

God deserves our devotion. He searches for us. We may think, because we have wandered away, God would prefer we stay gone; but His Word paints a very different picture.

> *"For this is what the Sovereign Lord says: I myself will search and find my sheep... I myself will tend my sheep and give them a place to lie down in peace, says the Sovereign Lord. I will search for my lost ones who strayed away, and I will bring them safely home again. I will bandage the injured and strengthen the weak" (Ezekiel 34:11, 15-16a).*

Our God is so merciful that, even when we fail to spend time with Him, He still pursues us. If we have trouble believing this, we need only open up our Bible to Luke 15, which tells the parables of the lost sheep, the lost coin and the lost son. It is the only time in Scripture where three consecutive parables deliver a singular message: God has not forgotten us, and He rejoices when we return to Him.

SEARCHING FOR AN ANSWER

There are also times when we are walking closely with the Lord, but still seeking His will for a specific situation. When I was going through my divorce, I was unclear about whether to sell my home and move to another state where I had family. My lawyer advised me to make the decision before the divorce was finalized.

I was torn. I had wonderful neighbors and friends where I lived, but knew there was no way to predict whether the court would allow me to keep the home we lived in. The desire to be where God wanted me was in my heart, but I wasn't exactly sure where He wanted me. I began seeking the answer from Him.

A few days later, I read Psalm 37. The most well known verse in the chapter is verse 4: *Take delight in the Lord, and he will give you your heart's desires.*

When I reached verse 11, "*The lowly will possess the land and will live in peace and prosperity,*" I realized it was already the third time in the chapter that possessing the land had been mentioned. I began wondering if God was speaking to me about staying in my home. I stopped reading right then and prayed, "Lord, if You really are using this Psalm to speak to me, I'm going to need it to be really clear throughout the rest of this chapter and mention the *possessing the land* thing again." (Maybe I shouldn't talk to God that way…because I sound kind of bossy…but apparently He understands my heart and decides not to rain down fire on me. Whew!)

As I read the rest of the chapter, there wasn't *one* more reference about possessing the land. Instead, there were FOUR.

> *Those the Lord blesses will possess the land (v. 22).*

> *Turn from evil and do good, and you will live in the land forever (v. 27).*

> *The godly will possess the land and will live there forever (v.29).*

> *Put your hope in the Lord. Travel steadily along his path. He will honor you by giving you the land. You will see the wicked destroyed (v. 34).*

In my heart, the answer was clear; God was giving me the land. We would be able to keep our home. My heart filled with joy, not because of His answer, but because He answered. My delight was in the Lord, and His Word was true, because He also was giving me what my heart desired.

Although we eventually did move four years later, the years we spent surrounded by friends were such a blessing to our family. The added benefit of searching out God's will for our family was the peace it brought during the difficult times. Instead of going back and forth in my mind, or questioning the decision I made, I could rest in the fact that God had supplied the answer for me, and His way is always best.

FOXHOLE CHRISTIANS

God is always in the business of drawing us to Himself. "There are no atheists in foxholes" is a popular quote meaning that when people are under extreme stress or extremely fearful, they will believe God exists and begin praying for a solution. Whatever it takes to bring you to God is what it takes to bring you to God. That may sound redundant, but there is nothing during our short lives here on planet Earth more important than securing your spot in heaven. Nothing. So, whether it's...

a war being waged around you,

a medical emergency,

a financial crisis, or

the failure of a relationship...

if it brings you back to Christ, that is the reason for the trial.

When I was a young woman, my pastor's wife told me, "God will do whatever it takes to get you on your knees. If blessing you keeps you on your knees, He'll bless you. If trials are what it takes to keep you on your knees, you'll face trials." I found comfort in this, mainly because I hadn't faced many serious trials yet. I figured I would master the blessing side of things, hoping I wouldn't have to go through the trials.

If you have read this far in the book, you are quite aware I didn't escape a life without a *lot* of trials. There was truth in what she told me, except I believe God wants us to learn how to seek after Him in seasons of both blessings and trials, and He will allow us opportunities in both.

A lot of foxhole Christians are out there, crying out to God only when the going gets tough. Don't let that be said of us.

> *Lord, in distress we searched for you. We prayed beneath the burden of your discipline (Isaiah 26:16).*

If we seek the Lord only in our distress, why wouldn't He keep us there? Imagine if you had a friend who called you only when she needed something from you. Would you really consider her a "friend"? God isn't looking to be there for us only when we need something—although He does want to be there at those times. He also wants us to seek Him out just to tell Him about our day or thank Him for always being there. Don't wait until you are in the foxhole, the *time to search* for Him is always now.

EVERYWHERE I GO, THERE IT IS

Have you ever purchased a new car? The minute you drive away with it, you start seeing the same car everywhere. *Were there really this many out on the road yesterday?* Or how about when you chose that super unique name for your baby and all of a sudden everyone seems to be using the same name?

The most likely truth is that nothing else really changed, except your awareness. You changed your focus from ignoring other cars and baby names to being conscious of them. Our subconscious is running in the background, catching what we might otherwise miss and alerting our conscious self of it.

The question is, what are our minds focused on? What are they searching for? Are we preprogramming them to search for God's blessings? If so, we start seeing blessings all around us.

*If you **search** for good, you will find favor; but if*
*you **search** for evil, it will find you! (Proverbs 11:27).*

If we search for the good in our spouses, children, neighbors and pastoral staff, we will find it. Our sinful nature is always quick to see when someone has done something wrong. I know when I am mad at my family, it's easy to compile a list of everything they do that annoys me. We don't want those around us focusing on what we do wrong, but it sure can be hard for us to offer the same consideration in return.

God's Word is clear. We are going to find what we are searching for. What are you searching for? Furthermore, the Lord will be searching our hearts. What will He find?

*But I, the Lord, **search** all hearts and examine secret motives. I*
give all people their due rewards, according to what their
actions deserve" (Jeremiah 17:10).

My prayer is that He finds me searching for…
opportunities to share the Good News with others,
times when my children make wise and loving choices,
chances to express love to others, and most of all,
more of Jesus.

*O God, you are my God; I earnestly **search** for you. My soul*
thirsts for you; my whole body longs for you in this parched
and weary land where there is no water (Psalm 63:1).

Please, Lord, help me to earnestly search for You with my whole body, mind and spirit. It is always *a time to search* for You and a time to be found by You.

Make It Personal

1. Do you wax and wane (go up and down) in your pursuit of an intimate relationship with God?

2. When has God used His Word to speak truth into your life? If you can't recall a time, ask Him to begin using it now.

3. Meditate on Proverbs 11:27—*If you **search** for good, you will find favor; but if you **search** for evil, it will find you!* Who in your life do you struggle to find good in? Ask God to reveal the good in them.

24

A Time to Speak

Whew! Finally something I am good at…talking! No two words about it….just two million or so. I think out loud and my thoughts are many—too many, if you ask some. The spoken word has such power though. It has the power to…

encourage,

share life experiences,

talk out solutions,

make someone laugh, or

pray God's Word.

As much as I love to talk, and believe me I do, there are also those times when God is calling me to speak up but I find myself struggling and at an apparent loss for words.

THE HOLY SPIRIT SPEAKS…USING YOUR VOICE

Have you ever experienced a time when you knew the Holy Spirit was speaking to you and asking you to say something? Actually, before we go there, let's talk about how we know the Holy Spirit is speaking to us. These are some of the ways I know when the Holy Spirit is speaking to me.

The thought to do or say something comes out of left field. This means I may be getting into my car at the supermarket, standing in line at the post office, or doing one of a million tasks I've done a million times before, but *this* time, I'm supposed to do something different.

My excuses and reasons (basically more excuses) won't quiet the Holy Spirit. It doesn't matter what I tell myself...I'm too busy, the person will think I'm crazy, someone else could do it better, or my personal go to—"I'll just commit to pray for that person...that's enough, right, God?" At any rate, God won't leave me alone. The thoughts are like bubbles rising to the surface in boiling water—they come one after another incessantly, and the only way to stop them is to submit and commit to do whatever God is asking of me.

Last, but not least, the request lines up with the Holy Spirit's nature. *"For the fruit of the Spirit is love, joy, peace, patience, kindness, goodness, faithfulness, gentleness and self-control"* (Galatians 5:22).
The Holy Spirit is not going to ask me to rob a bank or give someone a piece of my mind when they've made a mistake. However, speaking a word of love and encouragement to another soul with whom my world intersects...that sounds like Him.

Once I am aware it is a message from the Holy Spirit, it is a *time to speak.* Recently I was on a quick run to the grocery store when, on my way back to my car, I noticed an older gentleman outside on the sidewalk. He had a little area set up with a donations bucket. I smiled at him, placed some money in his bucket and got into my car to leave.

Immediately, the Holy Spirit began prompting me to go speak to the man. I had my key in the ignition, so the excuses started up in my head…

Wasn't the money enough?…Bubble

But I'm in a hurry….Bubble

Remember my family is waiting on me….Bubble

Bubble, bubble, bubble.

Nope, those excuses weren't going to work. The bubbles kept coming. I also happened to be leading a Bible study, *What Happens When a Woman Says Yes to God* by Lisa Terkuerst at the time, and the Holy Spirit was conveniently reminding me of my promise to say "yes" to God. I pulled the keys back out of the ignition, got out of my car, walked back to where he was and began speaking with the man.

It turned out he was taking a break from playing his saxophone. I asked him how he was doing and if there was anything I could be praying about for him. He got a big smile on his face and said, "Just that I would keep being able to do what God wants me to do." Then he showed me the list of songs he played. They were hymns. He played seven days a week at different spots around town.

A time to speak doesn't have to be a call for you to get on a stage or lead someone down the Romans Road to salvation. It may be a word of encouragement to a brother or sister in Christ whom you may never see again until heaven. It's not what we say as much as our willingness to say whatever God places on our heart.

SPEAK UP

The most difficult times for me to speak up have been when it involves discussing difficult topics with those in authority over me. Have you ever had to bring up an uncomfortable topic with your boss, pastor or parents? These situations are especially difficult for me. I typically try to avoid the conversation for as long as possible, until the agony of not talking overrides the discomfort of bringing the topic out into the open.

Asking for a raise was always one of those challenging conversations to approach. As a young woman I worked for a non-profit hospital, which was always trying to find ways to cut costs. They got into the habit of not replacing employees when they left, and instead just forcing others in the department to absorb the responsibilities. At one point, a co-worker of mine left and her workload landed on my shoulders. However, my own position already kept me very busy. After months of carrying both loads, with no mention of filling the position, I found it necessary to confront the director of our department with two solutions. The first was to fill the position, and the second was to give me a well-deserved raise for the increased workload. It took weeks for me to gather the nerve necessary to approach my superior. I stressed myself out, rehearsed my speech over and over, and prayed.

Speak up, women of God, speak up.

The day I finally got up the nerve and walked into his office, I was ready for a fight, positive it would be an uphill battle. Fifteen minutes later, I had a raise. Not because I had my arguments all cued up or because my debate skills saved the day. I had a raise because I asked for it, and my boss agreed willingly.

We can spend days, weeks or months stressing out about how to speak up to someone. I wonder what would happen if we chose to see those difficult situations as an opportunity for God to bring about positive outcomes in our lives. Maybe we would stop running from them. Addressing conflict is vital to our growth—spiritually, mentally, emotionally and maybe even financially. The next time the need to speak up is before us, let's remember that God is in charge of the results and doesn't want us to fear man.

> *For God has not given us a spirit of fear and timidity, but of power, love, and self-discipline (1 Timothy 1:7).*

Moses is a great example of someone God asked to speak up. Moses' first response shows he had a spirit of fear...

> *But Moses pleaded with the Lord, "O Lord, I'm not very good with words. I never have been, and I'm not now, even though you have spoken to me. I get tongue-tied, and my words get tangled."*
>
> *Then the Lord asked Moses, "Who makes a person's mouth? Who decides whether people speak or do not speak, hear or do not hear, see or do not see? Is it not I, the Lord? Now go! I will be with you as you speak, and I will instruct you in what to say."*
>
> *But Moses again pleaded, "Lord, please! Send anyone else." Then the Lord became angry with Moses. "All right," he said. "What about your brother, Aaron the Levite?...Aaron will be your spokesman to the people. He will be your mouthpiece, and you will stand in the place of God for him, telling him what to say (Exodus 4:11-14, 16).*

As we know, Moses became a powerful leader of God's people. I wonder though if he missed out on some blessings because his brother Aaron had to be his voice...until he became willing to use his own. Don't let the spirit of fear win. **Speak up, women of God, speak up.**

TIME TO APOLOGIZE

Everywhere I look these days, new home décor signs with a list of Family Rules are popping up. On almost all of them, I see a phrase about forgiving each other. Occasionally I also see a rule about apologizing. Subconsciously, I think we would rather forgive, because apologizing requires us to admit we are wrong. I did find one sign that admonished, *Be the first to say, "I'm sorry."* Imagine what kind of families we would have if everyone rushed to be the *first* to apologize.

Honestly, I had to learn the hard way how to apologize. God taught me in some very difficult times of my marriage to apologize quickly. The scene usually went like this...my former husband would pick a fight with me, I would remain patient and calm for a long while (though it seemed to be his goal to push me to the point of lashing back), then eventually, I would retaliate. Once I did, the fight would end.

The hardest part came after the fight. God convicted me time and time again that I still had to be responsible for my part of the argument. It didn't matter if my husband was 98% in the wrong and only 2% was my fault. God wanted me to own my 2% and apologize quickly, even knowing that the chances were that I would never get an apology for his 98%. Making the right choice was between God and me, not my partner and me.

The good news is that learning to apologize quickly under those circumstances has made it a lot easier for me to apologize now, whether I am 2%, 50% or 100% in the wrong. Quite honestly, it has made me a happier person too. By admitting I am wrong more, I feel happier. This is why being a Christian flips human logic right on its head. God's plan works so differently. Earthly logic tells us if we admit we are wrong, we have somehow lost something. Don't believe that lie. The only thing we lose is pride, and if we open up our Bible right now to practically any page in Proverbs, we will quickly discover pride is not something to hang on to.

> *First pride, then the crash—the bigger the ego, the harder the*
> *fall (Proverbs 16:18, MSG).*

In the light of day, we all know we aren't perfect, so it only makes sense that we make mistakes and need to learn to be okay with admitting them, apologizing and moving on. One of my daughters struggles with apologizing, so we posted a simple prayer next to her bed that I challenged her to pray every morning.

> *Dear God, Please help me to choose right today or admit when*
> *I am wrong. Thank you, Jesus. Amen*

We noticed a difference as she started admitting she was wrong. It was very difficult for her at first, but she discovered, as all of us do, that it gets easier with practice. No one is perfect. Holding ourselves to a standard of perfection is a great way to be disappointed. Allow yourself to make mistakes. Just be quick to apologize, and you will see God's blessings for your obedience.

Speak Up, Sisters, Speak Up

Make It Personal

1. Is there something the Holy Spirit is prompting you to say?

2. How do you know when the Holy Spirit is speaking to you? If you don't feel you know, ask God to bring clarity to your mind.

3. We all owe someone an apology. Who do you need to apologize to? Make a commitment to do it. I promise it won't be as difficult as you think.

25

A Time to Tear

Have you ever been tempted to tear open a present earlier than you were supposed to? I remember searching the house, looking for where the Christmas presents were hidden. My mom was smart though and wrapped things early.

Do you recall the childhood joy of wondering what was wrapped in the pretty packages under the tree? Remember looking for your name on the gift tag, picking up the gift to shake it, and trying to make a guess about what it might be? The patience required to wait was excruciating.

Christmas Eve always came…eventually. In our family, we were allowed to pick out one gift from under the tree and open it on Christmas Eve. Oh, the decision was agonizing! Which one should I pick? You would have thought we were training for CSI the way we four kids tried using our scientific process of elimination to determine which present was *the* present to choose.

Eventually, after my parents had tortured us enough…or more accurately, we had tortured them enough by asking over and over and over again if it was time yet, they would relent. Oh, did we ever tear into those gifts, which more often than not, turned out to be the pack of socks or underwear Mom had gotten us. Unlucky bunch of pickers we were. Needless to say, none of us ever became CSI professionals either.

God's Word tells us that He has good gifts for us.

> *So if you sinful people know how to give good gifts to your children, how much more will your heavenly Father give good gifts to those who ask him (Matthew 7:11).*

Some of us have left gifts under the tree, and it is time to tear them open. Our heavenly Father has wrapped them for us. Among the hundreds of promises in Scripture, we find...

the gift of wisdom...

spiritual gifts for the body of believers...

the gift of abundant blessings.

Don't let these gifts sit unopened and unused. Get excited. The day has arrived to open them and enjoy the good gifts our Father has for us.

To open the gift of wisdom, all we have to do is ask Him for it. This is a prayer I lift up regularly because I recognize my need. I am desperate for wisdom in my parenting, life decisions, and basically...everything. How many times a day are we faced with decisions? It's relentless; fortunately God's wisdom is limitless and available to us, if we just ask.

> *"If any of you lacks wisdom, you should ask God, who gives generously to all without finding fault, and it will be given to you" (James 1:5, NIV).*

To open our spiritual gift, we must first realize we have one! Plenty of great books or online questionnaires are available to help us determine our particular gifting. I have the gift of encouragement or exhortation, which I pray God is putting to use in this book. I urge each of us to discover our gift so we can be operating in it...nothing is more exciting than to use the gift God has given us.

In his grace, God has given us different gifts for doing certain things well. So if God has given you the ability to prophesy, speak out with as much faith as God has given you. If your gift is serving others, serve them well. If you are a teacher, teach well. If your gift is to encourage others, be encouraging. If it is giving, give generously. If God has given you leadership ability, take the responsibility seriously. And if you have a gift for showing kindness to others, do it gladly (Romans 12:6-8).

To open the gift of abundance, start with obedience. God asks us to bring Him our tithes and offerings and He *promises* to pour out blessings on us. I can't guarantee what kind of blessings, but I'm sure we can trust God to give us what is best. Many times as a single mom, I had a need; and God supplied not just what I needed, but over and above. Just recently, I needed a new phone but didn't have the funds to purchase one. After randomly entering a Twitter contest not even knowing the prize, I ended up winning the exact phone I wanted. God blesses us abundantly!

"Bring your full tithe to the Temple treasury so there will be ample provisions in my Temple. Test me in this and see if I don't open up heaven itself to you and pour out blessings beyond your wildest dreams" (Malachi 3:10-11, MSG).

Ready…set…tear open that gift!

ANCIENT TRADITION OF TEARING

In the Old Testament especially, we see multiple references to people tearing a piece of clothing when distressed. I always wondered why this was done, so I delved into the history. The Hebrew word for this ancient tradition is *kriah* (pronounced kree-ah). It is practiced today, but actually dates back to Job, the oldest known book of the Bible.

Job stood up and tore his robe in grief. Then he shaved his head and fell to the ground to worship (Job 1:20).

Jacob tore his clothes and dressed himself in burlap when he was told Joseph had died (Genesis 37:34).

Mordecai tore his clothes when he discovered the plot to kill the Jews (Esther 4:1).

Hezekiah tore his clothes when he found out the Assyrian King was threatening to destroy Jerusalem and mocking God's power (Isaiah 37:1).

Kriah is an outward display of the intense internal emotions of grief or despair. In the case of mourning, the act is performed by close family members of the deceased. It is done while standing, because standing illustrates strength even during a time of grief. The tear is made on the left hand side of the chest for a parent's death, and the right side for all other relatives. A blessing is also recited by the family as the tear is being made: *Barukh atah Adonai Eloheinu melekh ha'olam dayan ha'emet.* This means, *Blessed are You, Adonai Our God, Ruler of the Universe, the True Judge.*

This is a beautiful picture of how letting others witness and share in our pain can be a step towards healing. Regardless of how overwhelming emotions originate, we all need a release. Your preference for dealing with them may be taking a run, having a good cry or locking yourself in your closet to scream...I may or may not have used all of these methods a few times. Okay, yes, I've done all of these...well, except the running thing...I hope maybe, just maybe, one day I will choose a run as my outlet.

No one can hold it together all the time, and to be honest, it doesn't seem healthy to pretend to be a super-person who can. We all have cracks and tears, which leave us *imperfect* and, simultaneously, totally relatable. People that look perfect all the time never really are. The truth is that we all have dents, bruises and tears which make us human and in need of a Savior.

THE VEIL WAS TORN

I love the Bible and get especially excited when I see how the Old and New Testament work together to reveal God's perfect plan. It seems the more I learn about Jewish history, the more amazed I am by the Bible and God's infinite wisdom. Nothing is placed in it by accident, and He reveals multiple layers of meaning and purpose in events.

There is no more significant event in all of human history than Jesus' sacrificial death on a cross for our sins. At the same exact moment Jesus breathed His last breath, God also declared a permanent change in His relationship with us.

> *And Jesus cried out again with a loud voice, and yielded up His spirit. Then, behold, the veil of the temple was torn in two from top to bottom (Matthew 27: 50-51a, NKJV).*

The veil was torn in two. Although recorded in the New Testament, in order to understand this truly momentous event, it is important to take a look at what the veil meant to the Jewish people in the Old Testament. The veil separated the Holy Place from the Most Holy Place in the temple. The Most Holy Place was where the Ark of the Covenant, the golden altar of incense and the mercy seat were kept. Amazingly, God dwelled in a cloud over the mercy seat, which is why that area of the temple was the Most Holy Place or the Holy of Holies. Although priests were allowed into the Holy Place, only the high priest was permitted into the Most Holy Place once a year on the Day of Atonement. When he did enter, he was to offer a sacrifice, or atonement, for the people's sin. The exact instructions were given to Moses and set forth in Leviticus 15, carrying with them the consequence of death if they were not obeyed completely.

We all have cracks and tears, which leave us imperfect and, simultaneously, totally relatable.

The veil signified that man was separated from God because of sin (Isaiah 59:2). It is even more wondrous to think of the veil being split down the middle when you understand how it was made. Josephus, a first century Jewish historian, describes the veil as being approximately sixty feet tall and four inches thick; he also asserts that horses tied to each side wouldn't have been able to pull it apart. Yet, at the exact moment of Jesus' death, the veil was torn completely from top to bottom.

This is wonderful news for believers because we can now approach God directly. Nothing separates us from Him. Thousands of years of Jewish laws were meant to point us to the need for a Savior. Everything changed in a moment. No longer were true believers defined by regulations, but relationship. The torn veil brought the opportunity for anyone—not just Jews—to come directly to Jesus.

> *Tearing through the veil of darkness*
> *Breaking every chain, You set us free*
> *Fighting for the furthest heart You gave*
> *Your own life for all to see*
> *(Relentless by Hillsong United)*

Thank you, Jesus, for the sacrifice you made, allowing me…sinful, selfish me…to approach the throne of grace and receive mercy.

Make It Personal

1. What are some good gifts the Father has given you?

2. How do you release overwhelming emotions?

3. Take a few minutes in prayer to thank God for tearing the veil and allowing us full access to Him.

26

A Time to Throw Away

It amazes me how much stuff I can accumulate. During my twenties and thirties, we moved frequently. Many times it was only a year or two between moves. Surprisingly, no matter how long I lived in a place, it seemed I always had bags and bags of items to throw away or donate when it came time to relocate again. I eventually decided if we were moving and I hadn't opened the box since the last move, I probably didn't need it in the first place.

I can't speak to the rest of the world, but it appears the financial blessing we experience simply by living in the United States creates a "stuff" problem. I am not rich by American standards, yet after even one mission trip, it is easy to admit I live in a wealthy country and am indeed wealthy myself. We have running water, flooring, multiple bedrooms and air conditioning. We are rich, without a doubt.

If we have a roof over our heads—we are rich.

If we have food in our pantry—we are well off.

If we can afford to eat out—we are prosperous.

If we own a cell phone—we are wealthy.

Having so many possessions can blind us to what we really need. We think we *need* that new pair of shoes, or new car, or new computer. Yet, once we have them, we wonder why we are still left unsatisfied and craving more. Things will never satisfy for long, which is why walking closely with the Lord is what our soul requires.

NEVER THIRST AGAIN

When Jesus approached the Samaritan woman at the well, He asked her to get Him a drink of water and proceeded to disclose her secrets; for example, He knew she had been married five times before and was currently living with another man. I can only imagine that His clear understanding of her situation was both terrifying and fascinating.

They discussed the difference between the water she was drawing out of the well and the living water He offered.

> *Jesus replied, "Anyone who drinks this water will soon become thirsty again. But those who drink the water I give will never be thirsty again. It becomes a fresh, bubbling spring within them, giving them eternal life" (John 4:13-14).*

The woman at the well appeared to be searching for earthly love. Our thirst for more "things" or specific "feelings" can be unquenchable. When we find ourselves always wondering why we need more, it is time to examine our lives and see if we are thirsting and hungering after a mere temporary fix. Jesus provides us with a supernatural solution to our constant cravings— eternal life through Him. When we accept the free gift of eternal life that He extends to us, the emptiness we are trying to fill disappears and is replaced with a wellspring of life. Imagine Old Faithful in your soul. No more room for emptiness when you are overflowing with the joy of salvation!

As women, I believe our hearts are often in the right place, wanting to give of ourselves to our families and loved ones. In order to continue giving to those around us, we must be tapped into the "fresh, bubbling spring" that is Jesus. Our eternity is decided once we accept Jesus, but to keep the Spirit flowing into our lives, we must not let this temporal world distract us.

> *Therefore, since we are surrounded by such a great cloud of witnesses, let us **throw off** everything that hinders and the sin that so easily entangles. And let us run with perseverance the race marked out for us, fixing our eyes on Jesus, the pioneer and perfecter of faith. For the joy set before him he endured the cross, scorning its shame, and sat down at the right hand of the throne of God (Hebrews 12:1-2, NIV).*

Throw off *everything* that hinders? Throw off *all* the sin that entangles us?

I'm not a runner. I'm the opposite of a runner. Unless that means I am a walker, because I don't really enjoy that either. All I know is, I hate running. When I do attempt it, it seems that I hear the phrase *I....Hate....Running* going through my head over and over again with every step I take. However, I do have friends who enjoy running marathons, and knowing them is as close as I feel I ever need to get to running one myself. When in a race, they wear lightweight items and don't carry anything unnecessary. They get rid of everything that would hinder them from crossing the finish line and focus on running toward their goal with determination and perseverance.

Jesus provides us with a supernatural solution to our constant cravings.

I think some of us, myself included, tend to run the race God has marked out for us while still weighed down by sin and unnecessary burdens. Why? Why are we holding on to things that slow us down? Hebrews tells us to throw them off. Throwing requires action and effort. Imagine a baseball pitcher who refuses to pick up the ball because it's too much work. The Bible doesn't say just ignore sin or our past and they will never hinder us. God is telling us, in order to run the race the way He intends for us to run, we must make some conscious decisions to remove barriers that keep us from running our best.

Knowing we should throw away what hinders us is one thing; but first, we must discover what they are. Sometimes we are very aware of the burdens we are carrying around.

Sexual abuse?

Unforgiveness?

Abortion?

Regret?

Lack of repentance?

Other times, we are unaware of the hindrances we carry. Many times our friends, family or counselors may see what we can't see. Are we brave enough to ask what they see? Maybe they see the abandonment issues we won't admit, or the mental health issues we refuse to acknowledge, or the misplaced priorities we have allowed. Only when we know what hinders us can we begin asking God to remove it and heal us from the past so we can walk in freedom again.

PERSONAL STRUGGLE

One of my hindrances is disorganization. Oh, it's a problem...a pretty obvious one actually. All you have to do it take a look in my car, which I justify with this possible scenario: if I were stranded after an accident is some remote place, we could survive off of what is in my car for a good week. Water bottles, crackers, granola bars and extra clothes—I have it all. Yes, I understand the likelihood of this is approximately .000001%, but that's beside the point.

The truth is that I do see how my disorganization impacts my life and my children's lives in a negative way. We are constantly running around because

I have forgotten an appointment until the last minute…or maybe, just maybe, I've forgotten my child at school (which she will *never* let me live down.)

In order to run my best race, I will need to face down this perpetual beast and tame it. If I do, the ministry God has called me to will get a better version of me, with more focus on what God wants me to do next. I will have less stress and accomplish more with the time I've been given.

SHE SAID "I HAVE A PLAN"…AND GOD LAUGHED

Another thing I had to learn to throw away was my perfect plan for the future. As a young adult, God gave me a heart for adoption. I wasn't exactly clear on the how, who or when, but definitely had some ideas I was more than willing to share with God. After a while I started to think my ideas were His ideas. This usually gets me in trouble….and when I say *usually*, I mean that I *often* find myself running ahead of God, not looking in the right direction, and smash head first into the closed door in front of me. I'm positive God has gotten some pretty good chuckles out of my "plans." He tends to surprise me instead with a path I never would have expected.

Back to adoption, the original plan, *i.e.* my plan, was to have a few kids first. Then, once we were "good," experienced parents, adopt a child, perhaps internationally, who needed the love we could provide. You know, because we would be "good" parents by then. It sounds like a logical plan, but it wasn't the plan God chose for our family. Instead, when our first daughter was only twelve months old, God put a situation in front of us that led to us adopting my almost three-year-old niece. An amazing part of the story was that our whole church was going through Rick Warren's *The Purpose Driven Life* study together at the time. During the forty days of the study, we came to understand the difficult situation Jerilyn was facing, offered to adopt her, the offer was accepted, and she moved into our home from out of state.

God's plan meant that I had to throw away my ideas in exchange for His....which were, of course, the whole reason He placed adoption in my heart from the beginning. I never expected my eldest child would be the one we adopted. I expected to adopt internationally. Instead, the need surfaced from within my own family. I was also shocked at how it came about, since my former husband was the first one who brought up the idea. You see, I had told the Lord that my then husband would need to lead in this area if God really wanted it to happen, and he did. Thankfully...

> *"My thoughts are nothing like your thoughts," says the Lord. "And my ways are far beyond anything you could imagine. For just as the heavens are higher than the earth, so my ways are higher than your ways, and my thoughts higher than your thoughts" (Isaiah 55:8-9).*

The great news is that everything God asks us to throw away—our things, our known and hidden sins, our plans for the future—all pale in comparison to how He blesses us for our obedience. We can always trust that our Father has our very best interests at heart.

> *LORD, please reveal and remove anything in me that leads me away from you. Help me to see what you see and think what you think. Fill me with wisdom and strength to let go of the plans I create and to accept the plan You have for my life.*

Make It Personal

1. Have you experienced an "unquenchable" thirst for a thing or a feeling in the past? Anything currently? If so, replace it with Jesus. Anytime you feel drawn to it...pray, quote a verse, or sing a song that reminds you Jesus is enough.

2. What do you need to throw away that hinders or entangles you?

3. What plans have you thrown away in exchange for God's better plan?

27

A Time to Turn Away

White chocolate raspberry cheesecake.

Fudge Brownies.

Oatmeal chocolate chip cookies.

Must. Turn. Away.

Yes, I have a sweet tooth. It's terrible, and by terrible I mean that sweet tooth makes it terribly hard to say no to desserts. I hate that I can't eat treats every day. It especially bums me out because there used to be a time, not so long ago, when I could eat whatever I wanted and it just disappeared into thin air. Well, maybe not thin air, but it did magically vanish. I know that's true because it doesn't magically disappear anymore....it stays with me, resulting in, shall we say, an enhanced figure.

Sweets may not be your vice, but I would be willing to bet you have one...a temptation that rears its ugly head with promises of fulfillment or gratification. Me, I have temptations daily, if not multiple times a day.

I'm tempted to watch television shows I shouldn't.

I'm tempted to throw away every item on my daughters' floor.

I'm tempted to scream at drivers in my way.

I'm tempted. I'm tempted. I'm tempted.

We are all enticed, either by our own evil desires or by the most experienced tempter of all time, Satan. He's been playing mind games with us since Adam and Eve, and he definitely sees each of us as a game piece. His tactics haven't changed; he will tempt us to sin and as soon as we have succumbed, he will flip on us and begin accusing us. One thing is certain—God never does the tempting.

> And remember, when you are being tempted, do not say, "God is tempting me." God is never tempted to do wrong, and he never tempts anyone else. Temptation comes from our own desires, which entice us and drag us away. These desires give birth to sinful actions. And when sin is allowed to grow, it gives birth to death (James 1: 13-15).

Some days it is especially hard to turn away from temptation. For me, it's usually when I am on the heels of a bad day or week, or I am walking the victory lap for some achievement in life. So basically, whether things are going bad or going well, temptation can strike. One of the things I adore about God is His infinite grace, which always provides a way out of the temptation; I just have to decide to take it.

> The temptations in your life are no different from what others experience. And God is faithful. He will not allow the temptation to be more than you can stand. When you are tempted, he will show you a way out so that you can endure (1 Corinthians 10:13).

It comforts me to know I am not alone. The sins I am drawn to change as I grow older and hopefully wiser, but no matter what they are, I can rest assured they are nothing new to God. His grace is abundant, and even though I am called to turn away from temptations, God will never turn away from me.

THE COST OF NOT TURNING AWAY

I have also experienced times when I haven't turned away from temptation. The most difficult for me is the temptation to let my anger have full reign, more often than not against my family. One time, when Jerilyn was probably about four and well before we had a diagnosis for her condition, I remember getting so angry with her that I picked her up and threw her on the bed. She rolled over and ended up hitting her head on the wall.

One of the things I adore about God is His infinite grace.

I felt like the worst parent ever, and it breaks my heart to even recall it. At that moment, I was at my worst because my anger was controlling me. The fruits of the Spirit like patience, kindness, and gentleness took a back seat to my uncontrolled emotions. My child looked at me in fear, and it changed me. It changed my understanding of myself and what I was capable of doing. By not turning away from my temptation to lose it, I chose an out-of-control behavior, which led to shame, fear and utter disappointment.

An extreme example in the Bible, which illustrates the cost of not turning away, is from Lot's wife. You may remember the story. Abraham's nephew, Lot, and his family are barely escaping as the Lord rains down fire and brimstone on Sodom. In fact, the angels have to literally grab their hands and take them outside of the city. They had been commanded to, *"Run for your lives! And don't look back or stop anywhere in the valley! Escape to the mountains, or you will be swept away!"* (Genesis 19:17).

The rampant sin in Sodom and Gomorrah was shameful, and God commanded, through His angels, for Lot's family to not look upon its annihilation. Lot's wife was unable to stop herself from the temptation to look back and see the destruction of the city. Unfortunately, that image was the last she saw, as she immediately turned into a pillar of salt.

Lot's wife's actions teach us two things. First, obey God's commands exactly. Second, we do not need to revel in another's consequences for sin. An old quote comes to my mind: "But for the grace of God, there go I." I am no better than Lot's wife. Curiosity has caught me in its clutches before, but her example does remind me to keep my eyes and heart focused on the Lord.

SAYING NO TO RELATIONSHIPS

Although God never turns away from His children, there are times when we must turn away from someone in our life. Unhealthy and toxic relationships may require us to remove ourselves in order to protect our family or ourselves. This can be especially hard when the people from whom we need to turn are family members.

One of my friends comes from an extremely dysfunctional family background. At one point, this friend's legalistic stepmother began a campaign to isolate both this woman and her brother from their own father. The father cowered to his wife and refused to take a stand for his children. It got to the point where the stepmother called the cops when my friend tried to check in on her father.

No one except the Holy Spirit can tell you what the right answer is for you.

As difficult as it was for her, she was forced to make a decision to turn away. She longed not only for a relationship with her father, but also for his love and acceptance. Instead, rejection was the common theme. After much prayer, my friend recognized she had to turn away from her continual attempts to create the relationship she wanted to have with her father. She needed to protect herself and also her children from the constant rejection. She learned to look to God to fill the father hole in her heart. The good news is our Abba Father is the best daddy ever, and he is faithful to step into that role in our lives.

There are other times when we must turn away from acquaintances, friends or opportunities because they are drawing us away from the Lord. This is when it is most important for us to be walking with the Spirit so we can hear His clear direction. In the exact same circumstance, He may call one of His children to turn away and another to be the light in a dark place. No one except the Holy Spirit can tell you what the right answer is for you. Spend time in prayer and the Word, asking to walk in His will regarding the difficult situation. Trust God to speak to you and then obey.

VENGEANCE IS NOT MINE

Turning away from vengeance when you have been wronged is difficult for anyone. A story that inspired me was about a father who lost his teenage son in a random gang-related shooting. Initially consumed with the desire to see justice for his son, he threw himself into the court case and the eventual sentencing of the gang member. After the guilty man was behind bars, the father realized his anger was below the surface at all times. It wasn't until the parole hearing years later that he recognized he was holding on to the desire for vengeance. After the guilty man was denied parole, the father looked across the aisle and saw tears on another father's face. His anger dissipated, and he reached out to shake the other man's hand, who happened to be the father of the young man who had murdered his son. The two men developed a friendship over the years and traveled together speaking about gang violence and focusing on helping gang members find better opportunities. Turning away from wrath led to a forgiveness that impacted many lives in a positive way.

TURN AWAY FROM BITTERNESS

We may never face a situation as serious as the murder of a loved one, but it is extremely easy, and human, to let the ways we have been wronged by others seep into our souls and leave a wound. These wounds then fester and leave us with trust issues and bitterness—which is exactly what our enemy wants, but diametrically opposed to what our heavenly Father wants for us. It is hard to walk in the fullness of faith when weighed down by the hurts of the past, like...

a co-worker taking credit for your work,

someone purposefully hurting you or someone you love, or

your best friend turning her back on you.

Yes, we've all been wronged. Yes, it hurts. Yes, the offender deserves a consequence. However, our bitterness never does anything except hurt us more. Have you ever driven somewhere on autopilot and had trouble remembering how you got there? Bitterness is like that. It takes root, and we don't even realize it is calling the shots until we wake up and realize we are pretty far off track from where we wanted to be.

Bitterness can even disguise itself to look like your friend and protector. *You remember when 'we' did that before and got hurt? It's best not to risk getting hurt again.* It bubbles out of us in the jokes we tell, quick judgments, harsh feelings, blame, and how we let the experience steal our joy for a different future.

I have had to fight against bitterness taking root in my soul, and the best way I have found to avoid bitterness or to kick it out of my soul is praying specifically for the person who wounded me.

Heavenly Father, thank you for loving me completely no matter where I am on the bitterness scale right now, but I ask that You help me move to a place of true forgiveness for (insert name). Stretch my ability to love and forgive. I pray that he/she will have Your favor and blessing. I pray that (insert name) will be drawn into a real relationship with You and see the blessings of obedience. Hurting people hurt people. Heal (insert name)'s wounds from the past. Please use this painful experience and bring good things out of it, things I couldn't begin to hope or imagine. Amen.

Satan brought this pain to our doorstep, but don't let bitterness steal our future. Satan loves the domino effect of sin…if he can get one person to sin, it can lead to a multitude of sins. Stop sin in its tracks by turning away and refusing to allow bitterness any room in your heart.

Make It Personal

1. What is something or someone you knew you were supposed to turn away from, but didn't? What were the consequences?

2. Is there anything God is telling you to turn away from now?

3. When was the last time you turned away from something in obedience to God? What were the rewards?

4. Are you harboring any bitterness in your heart? If so, confess it and pray for the person who wronged you.

28

A Time for War

When my two oldest daughters were around four and five years old, we were driving around town running errands. As I glanced in the rearview mirror, I could see their sweet little faces and decided it would be a great time to sing a song together…very Mary Poppins of me, I know. I asked them which song they would like to sing. My heart swelled with pride as one suggested "Jesus Loves Me" while the other offered up "Jesus Loves the Little Children." As proof of my obviously good parenting, they wanted to sing about Jesus. My pride was quickly nipped in the bud though as the two began fighting about which song to sing first, and it spiraled into an all-out war with punches being thrown and both screaming for their "Jesus" song at the top of their lungs. Somehow I think they missed the boat on what Jesus might have wanted at that moment, because a war about which Jesus song to sing wasn't doing Him any favors.

As a child, I was often battling with my younger sister. We had, and still do have, very different personalities and approaches to life. What we had in common was our size, so our conflicts were usually over clothes.

As an adult, what I am willing to go to war over has evolved. Every time I head into a courtroom, I feel as though I am preparing for combat. It takes strategic planning, emotional energy and spiritual readiness.

I always pray Ephesians 6 before heading into the battle.

> *Finally, be strong in the Lord and in his mighty power. Put on the full armor of God, so that you can take your stand against the devil's schemes. For our struggle is not against flesh and blood, but against the rulers, against the authorities, against the powers of this dark world and against the spiritual forces of evil in the heavenly realms. Therefore put on the full armor of God, so that when the day of evil comes, you may be able to stand your ground, and after you have done everything,* **TO STAND.** *Stand firm then, with the belt of truth buckled around your waist, with the breastplate of righteousness in place, and with your feet fitted with the readiness that comes from the gospel of peace. In addition to all this, take up the shield of faith, with which you can extinguish all the flaming arrows of the evil one. Take the helmet of salvation and the sword of the Spirit, which is the word of God (Ephesians 6:10-17, NIV, emphasis mine).*

The phrase "on the day of evil" jumped off the page at me the first time I read it before my day in court. It was my "day of evil," and God was giving me clear instructions on what to do…"to stand."

Once we are prayed up…

Once we have laid our burdens at the cross…

Once we have prepared as much as we can…

Once we have done everything else, all He asks is for us…

TO STAND.

God holds everything in His hand. The same one who placed the stars in the sky and created the heavens and the earth is the one who is in control. He is asking us to "stand" because He can handle the rest.

Having God as my Father who has already determined the right outcome for me is a blessing. Notice, I said HE determines the right outcome; I don't. I may desire a certain outcome and pray for a specific result, but only God knows the right path for my family.

My girlfriend once gave me a coffee mug with the following quote, "I'm not bossy. I just have better ideas." It always makes me laugh. As the eldest child in my family, being bossy was a given. Of course, I don't *think* of myself as bossy, but I'm probably the only one left who doesn't. Although I'd sure like to boss God around some days and guarantee my desired outcome, I know I would be worse off for it. In addition, based on my past experience, He won't put up with that from me. God knows much better what my family needs. He sees all the way to the end of time. He knows the repercussions of every decision, every verdict.

God uses battles for His good purposes.

At times, my interpretation of events leaves me feeling like God has forgotten us. Yet, despite my faltering faith, God, my hero, swoops in and reminds me that He has a much better plan.

I've experienced both good and bad days in court, but my goal on the bad days is to stay focused on the promises God has given me and trust He has the better plan, even when I don't understand it.

WHO IS YOUR ALLY?

God uses battles for His good purposes. On many occasions in the Old Testament, God brought enemies to fight His chosen people as a way to draw their hearts back to Him. Other times, God commanded them to go into battle to display His glorious power. Hearts inevitably turned toward Him, whether in praise or in repentance.

God allows the battles in our lives for the very same purpose, to draw us closer to Him. Before heading into a battle, I want to be prayed up and repentant of my many sins. Humbling myself before the God I love, yet often fail, is crucial to partnering with the Holy Spirit. As Christians, we do not go into battle alone, and it helps if we've had some one-on-one time with our Ally. Imagine how devastating it would have been to the war effort during WWII if all of the Allied countries had not first discussed a plan of attack and instead said, "Hey, Soviet Union, France, Australia…we'll see you when we see you." Pretty sure that wouldn't have had a pretty ending.

HE IS COMING BACK

At this very moment, some countries are looking for ways to bring terrible destruction and war to our shores. Evil minds are conspiring to destroy our way of life. This can probably be said of many countries at any time in history, but none more so than Israel. Israel literally sits surrounded on all sides by their enemies.

We live in an interesting time, where it appears the rapture is imminent. Fellow Christians, we could be headed home to heaven any day now! Those left behind will face seven years of tribulation, which will end in a great war. In this war, no prisoners will be taken, no hiding place will be found, and no mercy bestowed. God will have given chance after chance after chance for people to repent and turn to Him. The only ones left here on Earth by the time Jesus returns will be those dead set against bowing their knee to the One True God.

The time to wait another day before making a decision will be over.

The time for debate will be over.

Time for any and every thing will be over.

This war will not be like any other before it. The entire confrontation will be finished with words from Jesus' mouth. In the same way He created the Earth with a few words, He will also end it all with His words.

This war is coming. It is real. The battlefield will be bloody. Now is the time to share with our friends the Good News that Jesus desires for them to know Him and be spared the consequences of a world that refuses to acknowledge God.

Sharing our faith can be difficult, but it also can be the difference between life and death for our friends and family. How can we possibly avoid what we may view as an uncomfortable conversation when it could save our friends and loved ones from a horrible war and, even more terrifying, an eternity separated from God? We currently have the freedom to speak openly about our faith, but we have no guarantees that these freedoms will always be ours.

I'm sure the Jews in pre-World War Europe felt their freedom to identify with their Jewish heritage and religion would never change. Unfortunately, it did and it became dangerous for them to do so. We see these same changes occur often throughout history. Countries rise and fall. Popular opinion wavers. During the reign of Nero, Christians were persecuted for their belief in Jesus. In our country, we used to acknowledge God in our classrooms, but now teachers risk getting fired if they mention God.

The time and freedom to make a decision for Him are gifts with an expiration date. God's Word promises an end to both eventually. This spurs me on to share with my family and friends. God has blessed us immeasurably.

He has called us by name.

He sacrificed His life so we can live.

He has a place prepared for us in heaven.

The hope in us is the light for this world. Let your light shine, my friend,

LET IT SHINE.

Make It Personal

1. When was the last time you felt you were heading into battle? Did you cry out to God?

2. Do you have an example of a time God used a battle in your life for your good?

3. Are you familiar with the final war God reveals to us in Revelation? If not, take out your Bible and study it. *"Blessed is the one who reads, as well as those who hear the words of this prophecy and pay attention to what is written in it because the time is near"* (Revelation 1:3).

Epilogue

Let's tie up a few loose ends here. Although I don't know the *end* of our story yet, I can tell you that my daughters and I are doing well.

My eldest daughter Jerilyn is now eighteen and in her senior year of high school. She has beaten all the odds. Hands down, she is the boldest evangelist I know. My prayers…namely that she have wisdom and for God to give her a double portion of joy…have been honored by a Father who loves her even more than I do. We live in hopeful expectation of the plans God has for her.

In 2015, I faced my biggest court battle to date, and God made it clear I was to represent myself. In ten years of court, I'd always had the buffer of an attorney. This time, I stepped forward in faith and let God direct me. It was stressful. It was a ton of work. But God showed Himself mighty and faithful. The judge removed all legal decision-making power and visitation rights from my former husband. We received the freedom we desperately needed and my daughters have blossomed under our newfound peace.

God continues to do extreme things in my life. One of the more recent examples occurred when I had an angel encounter, which will be featured in the second book of the When God Happens series by Angela Hunt and Bill Myers. I fully expect the challenges and miracles to continue because one thing is true; we have AN EXTREME GOD FOR AN EXTREME LIFE.

Appendix A

These are a few resources to help.

Depression

Families for Depression Awareness

www.familyaware.org

Sexual Abuse

National Sexual Assault Hotline

1.800.656.4673

RAINN (Rape, Abuse & Incest National Network)

www.rainn.org

1.800.656.HOPE

Suicide

National Suicide Prevention Lifeline

https://suicidepreventionlifeline.org/

1.800.273.8255

American Foundation for Suicide Prevention

https://afsp.org/

Acknowledgements

First and foremost, I want to thank my Heavenly Father who planted the dream of this book in my heart so many years ago, and then watered it in His loving and patient way. Any and all fruit it bears belongs to Him.

I never would have finished this labor of love without the accountability of my Abba's Writers group including Billi Joy, Cori, Jenene, Emjay, Vivian and the many, many others who read, edited, and encouraged me along the way. Thank you to each and every one of you.

A special thank you to Cori Orlowski, who pulled out a calendar and forced a writing schedule on me. Also, for the many times she opened her home to me for writing nights.

My friend, Sterling Raphael, who will be shocked to be listed here because I'm sure he has forgotten how it was his idea to place the chapters in alphabetical order and how that little idea helped me so tremendously.

My beta readers, who read through and gave me their honest and helpful feedback, were invaluable. Thank you Beth, Kelly, Julie, Jen, Aunt Susan, Heather, Jenn, Vicki, Thais, Robin, Amanda, Brittney, Megan, Jaimee, Jenene, Stephanie, Paulette and Joy.

My launch team, who helped put this book into the hands of the people who needed it.

Ethel Wisniewski for her support and encouragement.

Misty Pernot, Julie Davis, and Maureen Knotts, who walked me through the worst of the worst days showing me the tangible love of Christ and encouraging me to just take the next step. I would not be me, without each of you.

Last but not least, my family. My mom who always makes herself available to help, my dad who believes in me, my sister Julie who is one of my loudest cheerleaders, and my beautiful daughters;

Jerilyn, who teaches me that there is beauty in challenges,

Ainsley, who keeps us laughing along the journey, and

Daisy, who inspires me to be courageous.

About the Author

April Chapman is an inspirational speaker for Christian women's conferences and events. She loves to encourage women to be FAITH-FULL, even when the circumstances of life are overwhelming.

You can find April at:
www.April-Chapman.com
www.fb.com/aprilchapman.author